GREENHOUSE TOMATOES,
LETTUCE AND CUCUMBERS

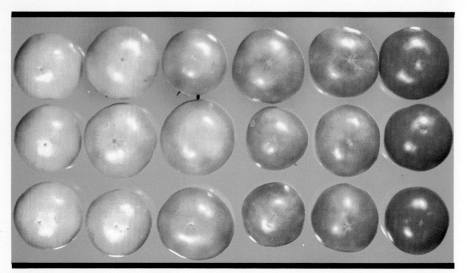

Frontispiece. *Color development in greenhouse tomatoes ranging from 10% on the left to 100% on the right. Consumers prefer fruit showing 100% or near 100% color.*

GREENHOUSE TOMATOES, LETTUCE AND CUCUMBERS

BY *S. H. Wittwer* AND *S. Honma*

East Lansing

Michigan State University Press • *1979*

৵ PREFACE

Greenhouse Tomatoes, Guidelines for Successful Production was published in 1969. The past ten years have witnessed dramatic new developments in greenhouse vegetable culture. Major advances have occurred with tomatoes and the production of lettuce and cucumbers has increased in importance. Marked expansions in acreage have occurred in Europe, the Far East, and the Near East. A once highly concentrated industry in the United States has become geographically disbursed. New structures have been designed. There has been a revolution in development of root culture media. The nutrient film technique has been created.

Completely programmed environmental agricultural production units ("factories") providing the optimal mixes of light, heat, nutrients, atmosphere, and growing media have been designed in the United States by two major industries—General Mills of Minneapolis, Minnesota, and General Electric of Syracuse, New York. General Mills is concentrating on lettuce production; General Electric on tomatoes, cucumbers, and lettuce. Biological control of some important insect pests is now a reality. An energy crisis and inflation have added markedly to the costs of production. Energy conservation practices are being sought, and the possibility for solar heating to reduce fuel costs has potential. New disease resistant varieties have increased production. Carbon dioxide enrichment is a standard practice.

A major part of this book is devoted to the latest information on the production of greenhouse tomatoes. There are also sections on greenhouse lettuce and cucumbers. Lettuce is commonly grown as a companion or intercrop with tomatoes. Crops of lettuce grown in the fall and winter months often precede a spring planting of tomatoes. Cucumbers may be grown as an alternative to tomatoes. The long green seedless and bitterless types, grown only in greenhouses, are receiving an increasing market acceptance in all producing areas in the U.S.A. and abroad. Many of the new cultural developments for greenhouse crops apply equally to tomatoes, lettuce, and cucumbers. There are over 100 illustrations.

Many friends and associates have contributed to the contents of this volume. Special thanks are extended to Richard Baurele, of the Ohio Agricultural Research and Development Center at Wooster; Hunter Johnson, of the University of California at Riverside; Merle Jensen, of the Environmental Research Laboratories, University of Arizona at Tucson; Arthur Loughton, Horticultural Experiment Station, Simcoe, Ontario, Canada; Frank Ingratta, Research Scientist, Horticultural Research Institute of Canada, Vineland Station; D. Rudd-Jones and Allen Cooper, of the Glasshouse Research Institute at Littlehampton, Sussex, England; and, Asgar Klougart, of the Horticulture Department, University of Copenhagen in Denmark. Some of the innovative ideas of Richard Pretzer and Al Gerhart, two outstanding growers in the Cleveland, Ohio area, have been emphasized.

While the above have freely discussed their ideas with the authors, they are in no way responsible for errors which may have crept into this book. For these, the authors accept full responsibility. Any listings of trade names of products, sources of seed, or otherwise are to provide information for interested growers. No special endorsement of the named products is to be implied, or criticism of similar products not mentioned.

ʂ TABLE OF CONTENTS

❧ INTRODUCTION

Greenhouse tomato production offers one of the greatest challenges in contemporary agriculture. Of all the food crops grown under glass, polyvinyl chloride (PVC), polyethylene plastic, or fiberglass, the tomato exceeds all others combined, in value and acreage. Conservative figures through 1978 showed a five percent increase in acreage per year in the United States—with installations extending from Texas and Hawaii to Alaska—and a ten to twenty percent increase per year in western Europe. In England, France, Italy, Belgium, Bulgaria, Romania, Hungary, U.S.S.R., Israel, Turkey, and Japan the increase in acreage has been phenomenal, with a severalfold increase since 1960. This is a remarkable development, especially because of the increasingly favorable competitive positions for outdoor crops and winter production in the southern United States, California, Mexico, the Canary and Virgin Islands, Puerto Rico, and North Africa. Winter and spring imports from Mexico to the U.S. continue at high levels (Fig. 1–2).

The Special Greenhouse Reports of the November 1967 through 1978 issues of the *American Vegetable Grower* reveal a continuing interest in greenhouse tomato production. This may be partially explained by the new techniques of manipulating plant growing and crop production; by the development of new construction materials and improvements in greenhouse design, including heating, ventilating and air conditioning, innovative cultural techniques; and by the new disease-resistant varieties. It is possible to successfully grow tomatoes, cucumbers, and lettuce in large chambers using only artificial lighting. The economic feasibility, however, has not

1]

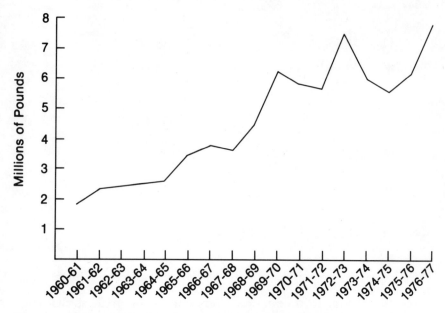

Figure 1. *U. S. imports of fresh tomatoes from Mexico (1960–61 to 1976–77).*

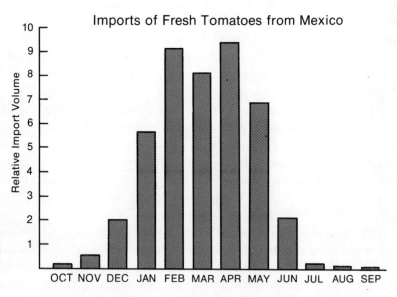

Figure 2. *Imports of fresh tomatoes from Mexico by month.*

yet been established. An effective sales promotional program for hydroponic culture has resulted in a phenomenal increase in acreage of greenhouse tomatoes and has also added fuel to what could soon amount to a re-awakening of the great potential in hydroponics. The

acreage of glass to plastic or PVC in the United States is approximately two to one, while in Canada it is three to one.

There have been ominous counter developments. While acreage
for greenhouse tomatoes in the United States has increased slowly, a
vast re-distribution of the industry is under way. Contrary to other
agricultural industries, production units have dispersed, increased in
number, and become smaller in size. Simultaneously, production in
traditional areas such as Cleveland, Ohio; Toledo, Ohio; Grand
Rapids, Michigan; Indianapolis, Indiana; and Boston, Massachusetts
has declined substantially and in some instances virtually disappeared. Acreage in the Cleveland area dropped 50 percent from
1965 to 1975. Many former growers of greenhouse tomatoes have
converted to flowers or bedding plants. Some greenhouses lay empty
during autumn months. When greenhouses are partially demolished
as a result of violent weather, they are not rebuilt. Bankruptcies,
foreclosures, and lawsuits are common.

It now appears that the life expectancy of viable greenhouse vegetable industries in the traditional growing areas in the United States
may not extend beyond 1985. The chief reason is the rising cost of
energy. The introduction and adoption of new technologies later to
be discussed could change the trend. This is now occurring in
northern Europe where the cost of energy is even greater than in the
U.S. Nevertheless, many commercial greenhouse tomato projects
have been initiated, and still are based on false economics and
promises of production goals which are never realized. A note of
caution is sounded. One is not going to get rich quickly in the greenhouse tomato business. Successful tomato production in greenhouses
is one of the most competitive, exacting, and intensive of all agricultural enterprises, and requires plant growing common sense. It is also
high technology.

Greenhouse tomato production technologies are more precise
than for cucumbers or lettuce. The initial investment is high. The
return on the investment, with no deduction for management or
the operator's labor, in the climatically endowed southwest United
States, is 4.7 to 9.7 percent. Labor is uncertain, expensive, and often
in short supply. Costs of heating have tripled in five years. Disease
and insect hazards are many. Air pollution is a serious problem near
many metropolitan areas. Competition from locally produced and
shipped-in tomatoes is always present, and is becoming increasingly
severe. It may not be easy for engineers to design and construct
greenhouses; chemists to formulate new plastics, fertilizers, and

pesticides; and plant breeders to develop new varieties. Yet, the greatest challenge of all is the consistent production at high levels of top quality fruit at times of the year when the demand is high and prices are favorable.

Yields of over one hundred tons per acre of greenhouse tomatoes have been produced from single experimental plantings at Michigan State University. Although the production yields obtained during a longer growing season in some European countries are greater, the yields of these experimental plantings are far above the average. Several new practices, some of which have already been enthusiastically adopted by commercial growers in Michigan, Ohio, Indiana, Texas, New York, Pennsylvania, New Jersey and southwestern Ontario, Canada have been responsible for these high yields. Growers will recognize that many of the plant growing procedures which are outlined here for the production of greenhouse tomato crops are equally beneficial for field plantings.

There is a continuing market for high quality greenhouse-grown tomatoes. Sustained acreage and expanded production into new areas reflect a potentially profitable industry. These suggestions are intended for the beginner as well as the experienced operator.

Prospective growers should familiarize themselves with the principles of successful production—good management, training and knowledge in crop production, and a continuing communication with successful growers and authorities in the field. Survival and expansion of a viable greenhouse tomato industry is contingent upon grower adoption of the latest in labor saving technologies, and use of structural materials, growing media, heating systems, and the conservation of energy. This book describes production practices that will enable growers to increase their yields of high-quality products, and do it with the least expenditure of high cost resources.

৽ SITES AND LOCATIONS

Many of the traditionally major greenhouse producing areas (Fig. 3–7) of North America (Cleveland, Toledo, and Cincinnati, Ohio; Leamington, Ontario; Indianapolis, Indiana; Grand Rapids, Michgan; Boston, Massachusetts) have become highly industrialized in recent years, and are no longer the most desirable sites from the

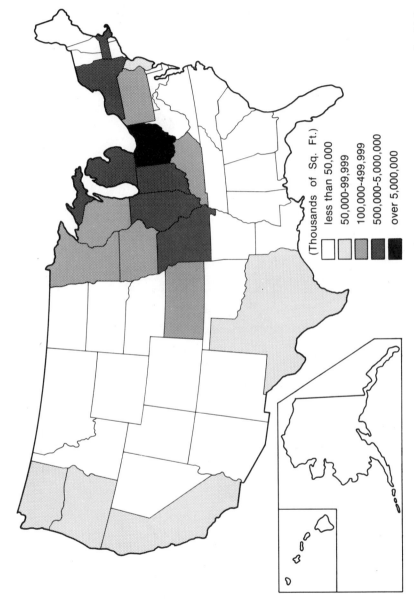

Figure 3. *Geographical distribution of the greenhouse tomato industry in the U.S. in 1959. Note the high concentration in the lake states of the north central region.* (SOURCE: CENSUS OF AGRICULTURE, SPECIALTY CROPS, U.S. BUREAU OF CENSUS).

(Thousands of Sq. Ft.)
less than 50,000
50,000-99,999
100,000-499,999
500,000-5,000,000
over 5,000,000

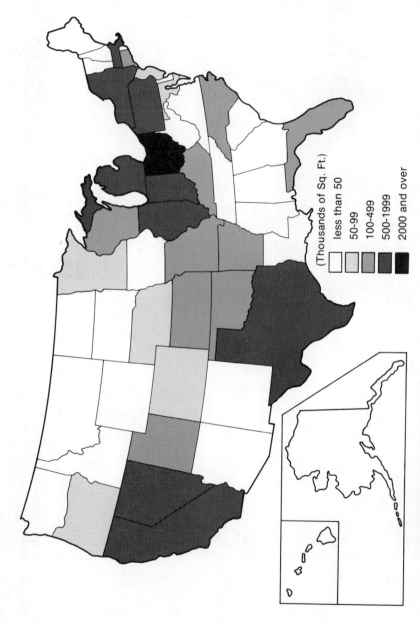

Figure 4. *Geographical distribution of the greenhouse tomato industry in 1969. Note the greater disbursement in the south and the west.* (SOURCE: CENSUS OF AGRICULTURE, SPECIALTY CROPS, U.S. BUREAU OF CENSUS).

(Thousands of Sq. Ft.)

less than 50

50-99

100-499

500-1999

2000 and over

[6

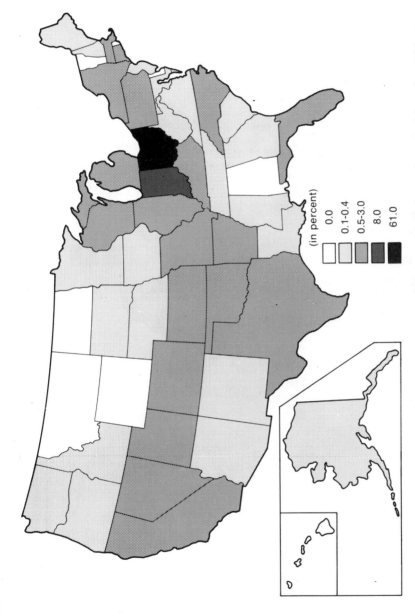

(in percent)

☐ 0.0
▨ 0.1-0.4
▩ 0.5-3.0
▨ 8.0
■ 61.0

Figure 5. *Percentage distribution by states of the greenhouse tomato industry in 1969. Note that Ohio pro-duced more greenhouse tomatoes than all other states combined.* (SOURCE: CENSUS OF AGRICULTURE, SPECIALTY CROPS, U.S. BUREAU OF CENSUS).

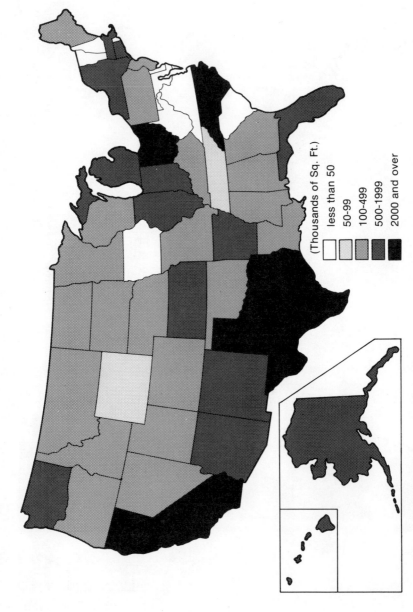

Figure 6. *Geographical distribution of the greenhouse tomato industry in the U.S. in 1977. Note the increasingly greater disbursement of the industry compared with Figures 3, 4, and 5.* (SOURCE: AMERICAN VEGETABLE GROWER, WILLOUGHBY, OHIO, NOVEMBER 1977, p. 13).

(Thousands of Sq. Ft.)

less than 50

50-99

100-499

500-1999

2000 and over

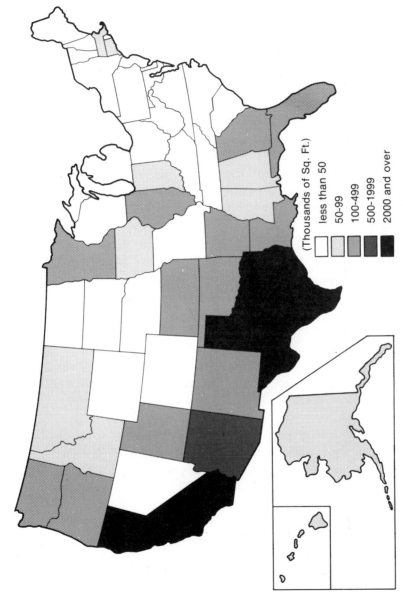

Figure 7. *Distribution of hydroponically grown tomatoes in the U.S. in 1977. (May include some lettuce and cucumbers).* (SOURCE: AMERICAN VEGETABLE GROWER, WILLOUGHBY, OHIO, NOVEMBER 1977, p. 12).

(Thousands of Sq. Ft.)

less than 50

50-99

100-499

500-1999

2000 and over

standpoint of land and water, taxes, labor supply, sunlight, and general air quality. Prevailing low temperatures and overcast skies during winter also necessitate large expenditures for heating.

Major geographical shifts and generally greater dispersement of the greenhouse tomato business has occurred during the past 20 years (Fig. 3–7). Production has greatly dropped off in many of the traditional areas (Ohio, Michigan, Indiana, Kentucky, New York, Massachusetts) and grown in other states (California, Texas, Arizona, New Mexico, the Carolinas, Georgia). One of the most significant developments has been the expansion of hydroponic culture. Success has varied from total failures to good operations. Many new greenhouse tomato installations have appeared in the far west, the southwest, the southeast, and the gulf states. The growing medium varies from traditional soil culture to artificial soil culture, block culture, peat culture, strawbale culture to hydroculture utilizing the nutrient film technique.

The most desirable areas for greenhouse tomato production should have a high sunlight intensity during fall, winter, and spring, mild winter temperatures, infrequent violent weather (tornadoes, high winds, hail, excessive snow), low humidity during summer for air cooling, cheap and abundant fuel, uninterrupted electricity, a good water supply low in salt (chloride) content, favorable freight rates, and most important, a good market demand either present or potential. Globally, such ideal conditions exist only in a few places and seldom, if ever, in the United States. The U.S. southwest has the greatest potential. Greenhouse tomatoes, however, can be grown successfully in many other areas.

Greenhouses may be oriented either east-west or north-south. Rows within a greenhouse may, likewise, be oriented in either direction. An east-west row orientation favors light exposure in midwinter. A north-south orientation would be most desirable during the spring and summer.

Some protection from cold winds will greatly reduce fuel requirements for heating. In the northern hemisphere, north or northwest exposures should be avoided. The natural soil type ought to be a well-drained sand or silt loam that can be easily improved by the addition of fertilizer and organic matter. Such soils would serve as an excellent base for sand, peat, sawdust, straw, or trough culture. Heavy soils, if well drained, may also be developed and can become very productive by the addition of large quantities of fertilizer and organic materials.

Irrespective of how or where a greenhouse tomato crop is to be grown, the availability of an ample supply of uniform and good quality water is essential. The salinity and soluble salt levels of the water should be low. In several European countries and especially in the western part of Holland, there is a shortage of good water for good crop production and, therefore, growers have begun installing water treatment plants to desalinize the water. Although the equipment is expensive, it is economically justified and is paid for in a few years. The Dutch desalination process is known as the "reverse osmosis" treatment and its use is on the increase.

High levels of chlorine in some municipal water supplies has proved highly toxic to greenhouse tomatoes and is corrosive to metals. Foreign materials or particulates can be devastating to drip or trickle irrigation systems if not removed by filtration.

❧ GREENHOUSE TOMATO VARIETIES

Successful production begins with high-yield disease-resistant varieties that meet the color and size requirements of local or distant markets. Although no accurate data are available, more than fifty percent of the varieties are F_1 hybrids (Fig. 8). The Michigan-Ohio Hybrid (MO–3, MO–7)[1] is the most widely grown red variety in the northern states. The WR–3, WR–7, WR–25, WR–29 [2], and Hoosier Hybrid are pink varieties resistant to *Fusarium* wilt, but not to leaf mold (*Cladosporium fulvum*). Ohio-Indiana Hybrid 0 [2] is resistant to *Fusarium* wilt (Race 1) and all races of leaf mold found in Ohio. The performance of this hybrid has been exceptionally good under proper culture and as winter and spring crops. Spartan Pink 10 has disease resistance comparable to that of the Michigan-Ohio Hybrid. Both Spartan Pink 10 and Spartan Red 8 [3] set fruit at higher temperatures and produce uniformly colored fruit with less cracking. They are particularly adapted for fall crops.

Tuckcross Hybrids O, V, K, and 520 [4] are red with 5–7 ounce

[1] Seed available from Roy Burghart, 6894 Lafayette Road, Greenville, Michigan 48838, and also from seed houses.
[2] Ohio Agricultural Research and Development Center, Wooster, Ohio 44691.
[3] Michigan Agricultural Experiment Station, East Lansing, Michigan 48824.
[4] Missouri Agricultural Experiment Station, Columbia, Missouri 65201.

Figure 8. *Hybrid seed production of greenhouse tomatoes is costly. It requires the hand collection of pollen from one variety and placing it on the stigma of the emasculated flowers of the seed parent.*

fruits. All are resistant to *Fusarium* wilt (Race 1) and to the most common races of leaf mold. In addition, Tuckcross K has resistance to root-knot nematode. Of the Tuckcross series, Tuckcross O is the most popuar, having found favor in certain areas of the midwestern, southern, and northeastern United States. It has good fruit quality and is tolerant to blotchy ripening. The Tuckcross Hybrids flower abundantly and may "overset" where conditions for fruit set are optimal. Where "oversetting" occurs, high yields of medium-sized fruits can be assured by heavy nutrient feeding and by controlled thinning, as necessary, of the less desirable fruit and late setting flowers of each cluster.

Tuckcross 533 is the most recent introduction (1972) from the Missouri Agricultural Experiment Station. This hybrid and 520 have larger fruit than the other Tuckcross Hybrids, and greatly improved resistance to all known races of leaf mold. Tuckcross 520 is used in plastic structures where leaf mold is a serious problem among hydroponic growers. Tuckcross 520 and 533 do not show the tendency to "over-flower" and "over-set"—typical of other Tuckcross Hybrids.

Several varieties developed at the Horticultural Research Institute in Vineland, Ontario, Canada (Veegan, Vantage, Vendor) and the Waltham Experiment Station in Massachusetts (Waltham Hybrid, Waltham Moldproof Improved) are available. They are red in color, resistant to several strains of leaf mold, but are even smaller in size than the Tuckcross Hybrids. Vendor is the most recent (1967) introduction from the Horticultural Research Institute in Vineland, Ontario. It is resistant to many strains of leaf mold, and has shown good resistance to tobacco mosaic virus in Canada, but not in Ohio.

Among the most promising varieties for greenhouses in the midwestern and southern states are the Florida group[5]—Manapal, Floradel and Tropic. Manapal and Tropic are large fruited, while Floradel is of medium size. All are deep fruited, red, and resistant to *Fusarium* wilt (Race 1), gray leaf spot, early blight, and several races of leaf mold. In addition, they are reported to show some resistance to growth cracks, cat-facing, blossom-end rot, gray wall, and tobacco mosaic virus.

The most refined for greenhouse culture is Floradel, and the most recent of the Florida group is Tropic (1969). A given flower cluster of Floradel sets all of its fruit within two to three days. Performance, thus far, has been excellent. Although Manapal and Floradel are still favorite varieties in many southern and western installations, the use of Tropic is on the increase. It is also the favorite in southern California, Nevada, and Arizona.

The Florida group of greenhouse tomatoes (Manapal, Floradel, Tropic) are generally later in maturity—up to two weeks—than other varieties. For comparable harvest times, scheduling earlier planting is necessary. A new F_1 hybrid of Tropic x Vendor is now on trial in Texas and Florida.

Several additional greenhouse tomato F_1 hybrids have originated in Michigan and have performed well elsewhere. They have re-

[5] Gulf Coast Experiment Station, Bradenton, Florida 33505. Seed is available from the Florida Foundation Seed Producers, Gainesville, Florida 32601.

sistance to both leaf mold and Fusarium wilt, and produce larger
fruit than the Michigan-Ohio Hybrid. These are the Michiana
series [6], of which Michiana 138 is best known. All are F_1 hybrids
of special strains of Michigan State Forcing and numbered Purdue
cultivars which confer the leaf mold resistance. Limited quantities
of seeds are available.

A recent introduction from the Michigan Agricultural Experiment Station is Moto-red (Fig. 9). It is resistant through most of the
life of the plant to Strain No. 1 of the tobacco mosaic virus. The
foliage is darker green, and the vines are more compact than the
Michigan-Ohio Hybrid; but the fruit maturity, size, and color are
comparable. The latest introduction (1971) from the same station
is the tobacco mosaic virus resistant variety—Rapids. The resistance
is comparable to Moto-red; however, it is not as compact in growth
habit. Rapids is earlier and produces as well as Michigan-Ohio
Hybrid. Heavy applications of fertilizer similar to that given other
varieties when mosaic symptoms appear are not recommended. The
vines will become over-vegetative.

Wolverine 119 [7] is one of the first commercial F_1 hybrids of
which Moto-red is one of the parents. Since then, several F_1 hybrids
originated in Michigan and have performed well elsewhere. These
hybrids are resistant to leaf mold, tobacco mosaic virus (Strain No. 1)
and *Fusarium* wilt (Race 1), and produce larger fruit than the Michigan-Ohio Hybrid, and are more compact in vine habit. These are the
Eureka series [6]. All are F_1 hybrids of Moto-red and special strains
of Michigan State Forcing, Manapal and numbered Purdue cultivars
which convey the leaf mold resistance.

Among the pink varieties are Ohio MR–9, MR–12, and MR–13 [8]
introduced by the Ohio Agricultural Research and Development
Center in 1971 and 1972, which are resistant to five Ohio strains of
tobacco mosaic virus and *Fusarium* wilt (Race 1). These varieties are
resistant to fruit cracking and fruit pox and high manganese in the
soil. The MR–13 has emerged as the favorite for most growers in the
Cleveland area. A 20 percent increase in yield is attributed to its
mosaic resistance.

[6] Roy Burghart, Eureka Greenhouses, 6894 Lafayette Road, Greenville, Michigan
48838.
[7] Holwerda Greenhouses, 612 28th Street, S.E., Grand Rapids, Michigan 49508.
[8] Seed available from Cleveland Greenhouse Vegetable Growers Cooperative Association,
19120 Detroit Road, Cleveland, Ohio 44116.

Figure 9. *Two important red-fruited greenhouse tomatoes. Left, Moto-red; Right, Michigan-Ohio Hybrid. Note the short compact vine of Moto-red. This variety is also resistant to tobacco mosaic virus.*

There are no acceptable greenhouse-adapted varieties available that are resistant to gray mold (*Botrytis cineria*), one of the most widespread and serious of all foliage and stem diseases afflicting greenhouse-grown tomatoes. Likewise, there are no suitable large fruited varieties yet resistant to nematodes, bacterial wilt, or bacterial canker. There are small fruited European types now resistant to both *Fusarium* and *Verticillum* wilts. Hybrids 7 and 9 of the Ohio Agricultural Research and Development Center are about ready for release. They are resistant to mosaic and both *Fusarium* and *Verticillum* wilts. If this multiple disease resistance can now be combined with resistance to nematodes, it may be possible to bypass the expensive and burdensome process of soil fumigation.

Varieties of greenhouse tomatoes differ considerably in their susceptibility to cracking or bursting. Emphasis on "vine-ripened" fruit makes any degree of tolerance or resistance an important consideration. No ranking of varieties as to cracking tendency is offered. It has been observed, however, that pink varieties are more prone to burst than are the red. Large fruit also tend to crack more readily than small.

ᕒ PLANTING AND CROPPING SCHEDULES

Correct timing in planting and cropping schedules is especially critical to the successful production of greenhouse tomatoes. It is very difficult and economically prohibitive in northern United States and Canada to produce greenhouse tomatoes for harvest through January and February. Sunlight during the preceding months and continuing through January is deficient and days are short. Fruit setting is sparse, ripening is slow, and quality is poor. Fuel costs are prohibitive, and heating facilities inadequate. Even for plantings which are seeded from September 25 to December 15, special care by experienced operators must be exercised in controlling growth during cloudy weather. Almost equally difficult and unrewarding is to maintain a harvest period through August and September. In addition to the preceding high summer temperatures which hinder fruit setting and result in poor fruit quality and low yields, the competition is severe from outdoor supplies which are usually of high quality and the volume more than adequate.

⊚   *The Two Crop per Year System.* This is recommended for tomato culture in greenhouses only where rigid disease control measures are practiced and possible. This system, does, however, allow for maximum production and utilization of labor. Plantings may be timed to avoid the adversities of high summer temperatures and low winter light intensities. Furthermore, it capitalizes on the highly productive status of the tomato plant during fruiting of the early clusters, and eliminates the battle with disease control associated with the many entry sites on plants that have produced many clusters of fruit. Essentially a spring and a fall crop are produced.

Many hazards, however, are encountered with the two-crop system. It is difficult to prevent mosaic virus transmission from one crop to the next, even though plant houses are isolated from the main growing areas. An additional mid-winter steam sterilization of the soil, to reduce disease carry-over, is expensive and may also release excessive quantities of nitrogen and/or manganese which unfavorably affect growth and fruiting. Planting schedules for both fall and spring crops are often delayed because of the short time allowed between removing one crop and planting the next.

Seed for the spring crop is sown from November to mid-January. Plants are set permanently from mid-January to mid-March. Harvest begins in March and continues until July. Normally, ten to twelve clusters of fruit should be harvested with yields ranging from fifty to seventy-five tons per acre. The recent precipitous rise in the price of fuel will encourage a delay in planting the spring crop.

The fall crop is seeded from June 25 to July 1. Plants are set permanently by mid-August. Harvest begins in October and continues until January. The plants are "topped out" in late October and, subsequently developing suckers are removed. Normally, six to eight clusters of fruit should be harvested, with yields ranging from twenty to thirty-five tons per acre. This two-crop system should result in the equivalent of a total yield per year per acre of seventy-five to one hundred tons of marketable fruit.

⊛ *Early Spring Single Crop.* This necessitates seeding from September 20 to October 10, and transplanting to permanent locations in November or early December. Harvest begins in late February and continues till August. Such an early spring crop demands the successful use of all of the latest production technology and superb plantsmanship. The current and projected high cost for fuel will discourage this planting schedule.

In the southwest United States, since sunlight is more plentiful than in the north, seed is sown from August first to September first, and transplants set in the beds about thirty days later. Harvest period begins approximately one hundred days later, and is terminated in May or June, depending upon the competition from outdoor grown products.

⊛ *Late Spring Single Crop.* This is, by far, the easiest greenhouse tomato crop to produce, and is highly recommended for the inexperienced grower. It is also the most energy conserving, and least energy intensive. Seeds are planted in late December or January, and the plants set permanently in the beds from late February to early April. Flowering, fruit setting, and fruit growth occur during the increasingly longer and sunnier days of spring and early summer.

Harvest begins in May and extends to August. Excellent crops of high-quality fruit are possible with plants producing from eight to twelve clusters with one to two pounds of fruit per cluster.

◉   *Fall Crops.* For the beginner, the fall crop is not recommended until the grower has been successful with the late spring crop, and is fully aware of the problems likely to be encountered in the fall crop. Initial fruit set in August and September is often hindered by high day and night temperatures. Although some means of forced cooling during August and September can be employed, the operation of the fan and pad system is beneficial only if the relative humidity of the air is low. In the southwestern United States where fall temperatures are higher, growers have installed pad cooling systems to obtain maximum production of high quality fruit.

Insects and diseases are easily introduced from the outside. As temperatures drop in late September and October, leaf mold and *Botrytis* become troublesome. By mid-October, there is no longer sufficient sunlight for good production, and fruit size and quality drop off sharply. Leaf miners and white flies can be especially troublesome pests for fall crops.

Inexperienced, as well as some experienced, growers in Texas, Arizona, Nevada, California, and elsewhere repeatedly attempt to carry a fall crop which begins fruiting in October or November through the winter months into the following spring and summer. This usually results in failure, discouragement, and prohibitive financial losses. The technology for maintaining a successful greenhouse tomato crop in which harvest begins in the fall and continues at a profitable level of productivity through the winter is not yet available. Carbon dioxide enrichment with an adequate supply of other growth factors may lead to the realization of this objective in future years.

◉   *Full Year Crops.* Another cropping technique in southeastern Ontario has been to grow plants for a full year. Seeds are sown in October. Harvest begins in February and fruiting continues through the spring and summer into the next fall. Diseases and handling of the extremely long stems present serious problems.

◉   *Intercropping With Lettuce.* Late spring tomato crops are often initially intercropped with lettuce. Lettuce plants, either Bibb

Figure 10. *Spring tomato crops are often intercropped with either Bibb or Grand Rapids leaf lettuce.* (ROY BURGHART GREENHOUSES, GREENVILLE, MICHIGAN, MARCH *1968*).

or Grand Rapids (Fig. 10), sometimes both in alternate rows, are set two to four weeks before the tomato plants. Spaces are allowed for the permanent tomato rows. The two crops may be grown together for two to five weeks. The temperature requirements for Bibb lettuce more nearly approach those for tomatoes, and it is more adapted to shading by tomato vines than the Grand Rapids type. Intercropping lettuce with tomatoes in late winter and early spring is an almost universal practice in the Grand Rapids, Michigan area and occasionally in the vicinity of Cleveland, Ohio. Lettuce with tomatoes necessitates a compromise as to optimal temperatures for either crop, but intercropping has consistently proven profitable in some areas.

A disadvantage to this system is that many of the fruits on the first and second flower clusters may be rough and incidence of blossom-end rot is often high. The low temperatures (below 60°F) necessary to grow the lettuce crop reduce pollen production and fruit set of the first clusters of tomatoes. Low temperatures do not influence the female portions of the flower, but drastically reduce pollen formation. Little or no pollen is produced at temperatures below 60°F. Growers tend to apply inadequate water to meet the needs of the young tomato plants in an effort to control the growth of the lettuce, thereby encouraging blossom-end rot of the developing fruits.

৯ SEED TREATMENT, SOWING SEEDS, AND GERMINATION

Tomato seed may be treated for tobacco mosaic virus on the seed coat without a loss in germination. A ten percent solution of trisodium phosphate is adequate. The seed is soaked in the mixture for fifteen to twenty minutes, thoroughly rinsed and dried.

Seeds should be sown in flats of soil, peat, vermiculite, or in mixtures of sand, soil, peat, and vermiculite and sprinkled lightly with water. Old flats and pots and soil should be thoroughly sterilized by steam heating before using. Rapid drying of the seed can be prevented after seeding by covering the flats with clear plastic or a pane of glass. The seed flats can then be placed above steam pipes or in any convenient location (boiler room) where the temperatures are from 65 to 75°F. Electric rubber mats[9] may also be used for rapid uniform germination.

Maximum light should be provided as soon as possible after germination begins. An alternative method, both for rapid seed germination and light, is to use 400-Watt infrared lamps above the seed flats. This enables seed germination even when air temperatures are kept at 55°F or lower for cold treatment of other seedlings in the same house.

There are two common errors in sowing tomato seed: sowing too thickly or too shallow. Shallow sowing, or a very light, loose medium,

---

[9] Available from Famco, Inc., 300 Lake Road, Medina, Ohio 44256.

allows seedlings to emerge with the seed coats still attached. This distorts the seed leaves (cotyledons) and sometimes the first true leaves. The use of a pane of glass or sheet of clear plastic, as mentioned above, will help in reducing moisture loss, and also assist in keeping the seed coat soft enough to allow the cotyledons to emerge normally.

When the cotyledons (seed leaves) are fully expanded and the first true leaf is visible, the seedlings are transplanted (Fig. 11). Although delayed pricking out of seedlings permits a better selection of better plants, it also increases the risk of transmission of virus from the diseased plants. In such an instance, remove the diseased plants prior to transplanting. Prior to pricking out, spray the seedlings with whole milk or reconstituted skim milk containing one teaspoon of detergent or sticker to reduce virus transmission. Allow the solution to dry for a few hours. This will protect the plants from virus infection for twenty-four hours. Be sure to wash your hands thoroughly with soap and water or in a ten percent tri-sodium phosphate solution before pricking out. Any equipment used in

Figure 11. *Tomato seedlings started in flats and at a suitable size for transplanting and the initiation of the cold "treatment."* (GORTSEMA BROTHERS, GRAND RAPIDS, MICHIGAN, FEBRUARY *1968*).

Figure 12. *Two to four weeks prior to permanent setting, plants in pots should be spaced progressively farther apart as they grow to avoid touching or overlapping of leaves.* (ROY BURGHART GREENHOUSES, GREENVILLE, MICHIGAN, MARCH, *1968*).

transplanting such as a dibble should be soaked in the ten percent tri-sodium phosphate solution prior to using.

Plants for the main spring crops are usually grown till near flowering in four-inch clay or plastic pots, peat pots, soil blocks, or in ground beds or in benches. Where ground beds or benches are used, the initial pricking is spaced approximately two inches apart between plants and between rows. Plants are pricked out again when they are two to three inches high. For plants grown in pots or

Figure 13. *Blocks of artificial soil mix make an excellent root growing medium that is lightweight and prevents root damage in transplanting.*

soil or artificial mix blocks, the containers are placed on plastic lined beds to control root development and spaced progressively farther apart as the plants grow (Fig. 12). Crowding which results in touching or overlapping of the leaves of neighboring plants should be avoided. Crowded plants will become spindly and tall. This type of spacing can be most conveniently managed with clay or plastic pots.

Peat pots can also be used if they are moved only when dry. Peat pots are becoming increasingly popular for growing plants for fall crops where wide spacing before transplanting is not practiced and the plants are transplanted at an early growth stage. Since they are not re-used, storage and sterilization problems are reduced or eliminated. Open bottom containers (bands) have not been accepted, as they do not confine the roots, and moisture levels cannot be controlled. Soil blocks are used extensively in the Leamington, Ontario, Canada area, but have not met with favor elsewhere. Blocks of artificial soil mixes have also been formulated (Fig. 13).

An alternative to seed flats and transplanting is direct seeding into pots or other containers which eliminates handling the young plants and the spread of tobacco mosaic virus. The plants can then be grown without personal contact until transplanted permanently into ground beds. Direct seeding into pots also results in more rapid growth and the earlier development of seedlings. Many growers, however, to conserve space and heat, prefer to seed into flats, "double-root" the plants by "pricking-off" the seedlings first into the beds spaced 1 x 1″ and later into pots, bands, or other containers.

The latest trend has been the complete elimination of containers in plant growing. Soil or peat blocks are still used, but most seedlings are transplanted, with appropriate spacing, into a growing media in beds, benches, or special boxes (Fig. 14). Some highly mechanized operations have been designed in the Cleveland, Ohio area (Fig. 15).

ࣔ PLANT GROWING

Flowers are formed in the tomato plant three to four weeks before the first flower buds are visible (Fig. 16). For the first clusters, this is within a ten-day to three-week period following the unfolding of the seed leaves (cotyledons). During this time, known as the sensitive period, temperature, moisture, light intensity and duration, carbon dioxide levels in the greenhouse atmosphere, and the mineral nutrient supply in the root medium are very important. Certain chemical treatments also exert a profound influence. The position of the first flower cluster in relation to the number of leaves on the stem is determined within a few days after the seed leaves unfold (Fig. 16.)

⊛ *Temperature Requirements and the Cold Treatment.* The usual growing temperatures for tomato seedlings range from 60 to 65°F. When outside temperatures permit, however, plants should be given the cold treatment. This means exposing young tomato seedlings just after the seed leaves unfold (Fig. 16) to temperatures 52 to 56°F for ten days to three weeks. Cold temperatures during both day and night are effective. Ten days are sufficient in bright, sunny weather; three weeks are necessary in cloudy, dark, or winter weather. The duration of the cold treatment is determined by the time required for the plant to develop to the two-leaf stage. The optimum temperature for the tomato plant varies with the stage of plant development (Table 1). Tomato plants properly exposed to a cold treatment develop large cotyledons and thick stems, with fewer leaves formed before the first flower cluster, up to double the number of flowers in the first, and often the second clusters, and higher

Figure 14. *Tomato seedlings may be transplanted directly into ground beds or benches. This eliminates the use of containers in plant growing. Plastic liners will prevent root growth into the soil below.*

Figure 15. *Special highly mechanized plant growing operations have been developed, using boxes prepared from sheets of plywood.* (COURTESY RICHARD PRETZER, CLEVELAND, OHIO).

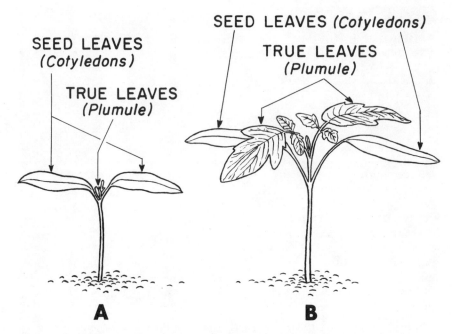

SEED LEAVES
(Cotyledons)

TRUE LEAVES
(Plumule)

SEED LEAVES (Cotyledons)

TRUE LEAVES
(Plumule)

A   **B**

Figure 16. *Diagrams (life size) of tomato seedlings. A, left, cold treatment for increasing flower number in the first cluster should begin at this stage, and continue until B, right, when the true (plumule) leaves are approximately one inch long. Flowers for the first cluster are formed during these two stages in seedling growth.*

early and total yields. The magnitude of the effect depends on the season or planting date (Table 2.) The Michigan-Ohio and Michiana and Eureka Hybrids and related varieties are particularly responsive to the cold treatment (Figs. 17–18). The increase in flower number is reflected in greater yields of fruit, not only in the first cluster (Fig. 19), but in later clusters as well (Fig. 20, Table 3). Some varieties such as WR–25 and Ohio-Indiana Hybrid O develop a considerable amount of rough fruit when exposed to temperatures below 58°F during the sensitive flower-forming period. The effectiveness of the cold treatment depends on the variety.

Simultaneous exposure of tops and roots of the same Michigan-Ohio Hybrid tomato seedlings to different temperatures has revealed that top temperatures determine the number of leaves that develop before the first flower cluster. Cold treatment of tops during the sensitive period significantly reduces the number of leaves before the appearance of the first flower cluster; cold treatment of roots greatly increases the number of flowers in the first cluster.

TABLE 1. Night and day temperature schedules, from seed germination
to fruiting, for the production of a spring crop of greenhouse
tomatoes.

Growth stages	Sunlight conditions	Recommended temperatures in degrees Fahrenheit [a]	
		Night	*Day*
Seed germination	Not critical	65 to 70	65 to 70
After cotyledon expansion (Fig. 16A) begin the cold treatment and continue for:			
10 days to 2 weeks during	Sunny or partly cloudy days	52 to 56	55 to 60
2 to 3 weeks during	Cloudy or dull days	52 to 56	55 to 58
After the cold treatment and until the plants are	Sunny or partly cloudy days	58 to 62	65 to 75
transplanted into beds:	Cloudy or dull days	58 to 60	60 to 62
During flowering and fruiting when outdoor conditions permit control	Sunny or partly cloudy days	60 to 65	65 to 75
of greenhouse temperatures by ventilation:	Cloudy or dull days	60 to 62	60 to 62

[a] Air temperatures recorded at average plant level. Soil (root) temperatures may be even
more critical than air temperatures during the early growth stages. For young plants
root temperatures should be close to the listed air temperatures. The ranges in night
and day temperatures given to accommodate slight differences among varieties. For
example, the Ohio Pink Globe selections (WR–7, WR–25, WR–29, Ohio–Indiana Hybrid
O) have a slightly higher temperature requirement than the Michigan–Ohio Hybrid,
Michiana 138, Wolverine 119 and the Tuckcross Hybrids.

Recommendations for the cold treatment of tomato seedlings
follow. The cold treatment should be started just as the first true
leaves emerge (Fig. 11 and 16), whether the seedlings are still in seed
rows or pricked-off. Air and soil temperatures should be lowered to
52 to 56°F for ten days to three weeks. A ten- to twelve-day cold
treatment is adequate during periods of good sunlight. Three weeks
are usually necessary in the fall and early winter when most of the
days are cloudy and plant growth is slow. The amount of cold
during the critical ten-day to three-week period is more important
than the time of day in which it is given. Cold exposure during
either the day or night, or both, is effective. Night temperatures of

TABLE 2. Effects of cold treatment of Michigan-Ohio tomato seedlings and time of planting on the number of leaves before the first flower clusters and the number of flowers in the first clusters.

	Leaves before 1st cluster		Flowers in 1st cluster	
Planting date	Continuous (60–65°F)	Cold treatment (52–54°F)	Continuous (60–65°F)	Cold treatment (52–54°F)
October 9	7.5	6.0	6.2	11.7
October 30	9.3	6.4	5.4	6.8
December 2	9.4	7.9	5.2	7.3
January 6	7.7	6.8	6.5	10.6
February 3	7.1	6.2	6.5	12.4

52 to 56°F are recommended when the days are sunny and partly cloudy.

Following the cold treatment, night temperatures should be raised to 58 to 62°F. Cool daytime temperatures (60 to 62°F) should be maintained in cloudy dull weather. On bright sunny or partly cloudy days, temperatures of 65 to 75°F accompanied by good ventilation are suggested (Table 1).

⊚ *Light Intensity and Duration.* Tomato plants started during the late fall or winter months should be exposed to as much light as

TABLE 3. Pounds of marketable fruit harvested from 8 clusters as affected by cold treatment of seedlings of Michigan–Ohio Hybrid and Ohio WR–7 Globe tomatoes.

	Michigan–Ohio Hybrid		Ohio WR–7	
Cluster number	No cold treatment	Cold treatment	No cold treatment	Cold treatment
1	2.0	2.6	2.1	2.4
2	2.2	2.6	2.3	2.4
3	1.9	2.2	2.2	2.3
4	2.1	2.7	1.9	2.1
5	1.7	2.3	1.9	1.9
6	2.0	2.4	1.9	2.1
7 & 8	3.7	4.1	3.4	3.9
Total yields (lbs/plant)	15.6	18.9[a]	15.7	17.1[a]

[a] Fruit yields significantly greater than those not given the cold treatment.

Figure 17. *The position of the first flower cluster, in relation to the number of leaves on the stem and the number of flowers in the first cluster, is temperature dependent. Left, Michigan-Ohio Hybrid plant maintained at 62–65°F night temperature. Right, the same, except exposed to 53–55° during the interval of growth illustrated in Figure 16.*

Figure 18. *Large flower-fruit clusters induced in the Michigan-Ohio Hybrid by "cold-treatment" of seedlings.*

Figure 19. *Large flower clusters induced by cold treatment of Michigan-Ohio Hybrid tomato seedlings can result in large fruit clusters.*

Figure 20. *Cold treatment of young tomato seedlings also enhances the productivity of later formed fruit clusters.* (ROY BURGHART GREENHOUSES, GREENVILLE, MICHIGAN, JUNE 5, 1968).

possible during normal daylight hours. Artificial lights, if used, should be employed only during the daylight hours on dark cloudy days, and should not be used at night to extend the length of day. The tomato is a facultative short day plant which flowers and fruits earliest if the day is not extended beyond twelve hours by artificial light. Young tomato plants do not need the light intensities of full sunlight. Where there is no overlapping of leaves, light saturation is reached at intensities from two to three thousand foot candles, or about one-fifth to one-third the intensity of direct sunlight at high noon. If artificial lights are used, an intensity of at least five hundred foot candles should be provided at the leaf surface. Tests with fluorescent fixtures reveal that the Wide Spectrum Gro Lux (Sylvania) is slightly superior to cool white.

If efficiency is measured by the amount of plant growth per watt of power used, the metal halide and high pressure sodium vapor lamps are more efficient than the standard mercury or mercury fluorescent or fluorescent lamps. The disadvantage is the initial cost of the lamps.

If the days are short (nine hours of light), the tomato plant will flower earlier and form the first cluster after fewer leaves than if day lengths are twelve or eighteen hours (Table 4). An increase in light intensity also hastens flowering (Fig. 21).

The data in Table 2 show that there were more leaves and fewer flowers on seedlings grown from late October through early December than from those grown after January 1. Tomato plants produced fewer flowers when the light intensity was low. The cold treatment for increasing flower numbers on plantings grown under low light intensities was less effective than when sunlight was plentiful.

TABLE 4. Effects of daylength and light intensity on the number of leaves that formed before the first flower cluster in the Michigan–Ohio Hybrid tomato that was simultaneously given the cold treatment.

Daylength (hours)	Light intensity (foot candles)		
	750	1500	3000
9	8	7	5
12	8	7	6
18	9	8	6

Figure 21. *Effect of photoperiod and light intensity on flowering of the Michigan-Ohio Hybrid tomato. Left to right, 9-hour photoperiod and 3,000 foot-candles; 12-hour photoperiod and 1,500 foot-candles; 18-hour photoperiod and 750 foot-candles. Note the position of the first inflorescence by arrows, relative to leaf number and the degree of floral development.*

Supplementary light (sodium vapor providing 6.3 watts per square feet or approximately 1000 foot candles) on seedlings from pricking-off to transplanting to the ground bed increased the early yield of certain cultivars, but had no effect on others (Table 5). For three of the five cultivars, the total yield (12 weeks of harvest) was more for those not receiving supplementary light.

The use of supplementary artificial light at the present time is economically feasible only for the growing of seedlings, since a greater number of plants can be illuminated per square foot. Small seedlings occupying a limited area are usually given twelve hours of high intensity light (800 to 1200 foot candles) daily for a three-week to four-week period. Many high intensity lamps for lighting of seedlings have been developed. Some have internal reflectors. They are extensively used for wintertime lighting of seedlings in Northern and Eastern Europe and in the Soviet Union during the short low light intensity days of mid-winter (Fig. 22). There is no advantage in using low intensity (25 to 100 foot candles) incandescent lamps on tomato plants in mid-winter to extend the daylight period.

⊛ *Carbon Dioxide Enrichment.* Carbon dioxide concentrations ambient to plant foliage remain the most important rate-determinant for further increases in photosynthesis and possibly yield. No

Figure 22. *Banks of high intensity lamps with internal reflectors are used for lighting of tomato seedlings during the winter months in the Soviet Union.*

exception to increased growth from CO_2 enrichment have yet been reported. It is no longer necessary to design and conduct experiments to establish the efficacy of CO_2 enrichment for increasing yields of greenhouse tomatoes when the atmosphere can be contained. The magnitude of the CO_2 response is light dependent, but beneficial effects are derived over a wide spectrum of light intensities—either daylight or artificial. Many experiments have now demonstrated that the optimum CO_2 concentration ranges between 1000 and 1500 ppm. This is three to five times greater than the current outdoor atmospheric level.

Young tomato plants are especially responsive to extra carbon dioxide in the greenhouse atmosphere. They have a higher optimal requirement than older plants. Growth rates can be increased by fifty percent, and early flowering and fruiting are accelerated by a week or ten days. Effects are carried into the fruiting period.

Beginning with a previously acceptable performance level in plant growth and development a greater increase has been obtained from carbon dioxide enrichment of the greenhouse atmosphere than from any other factor. All tomato varieties respond, including the new disease resistant types. The suggested level of enrichment is from 1000 to 1200 ppm. Not only is top growth and flower formation accelerated, but root growth is promoted even more. Carbon dioxide can be very effectively used as a potent growth factor to partially compensate for a lack of sunlight in propagating strong-rooted tomato plants for the early spring crop. Particularly promising is extra carbon dioxide in combination with artificial lighting. Carbon dioxide enrichment is also of special significance in hydroponic culture, since one of the sources of the gas, decaying organic matter in the soil, is not present. All plant growing structures now existing or those to be constructed should be designed with the capability of carbon dioxide enrichment of the plant growing atmosphere during the daylight hours.

Carbon dioxide enrichment gives the greatest dividends in the production of spring crop greenhouse tomatoes during the early growing period (Fig. 23). It is from the time the seedlings are pricked-off until the plants are set in their permanent beds. Light intensities during this period are usually low and carbon dioxide is a good partial substitute. Supplemental carbon dioxide also promotes

TABLE 5. Effect of supplemental light from pricking-off to transplanting on yield of greenhouse tomatoes at 5 weeks and 12 weeks of harvest. (Late spring crop, 1970)

Cultivar	Supplemental Light	Cumulative marketable fruit yield (lbs.) plant	
		5 Weeks	12 Weeks
Michigan–Ohio hybrid	+	3.69	12.53
	−	3.18	12.41
Vendor	+	3.53	7.93
	−	3.05	8.63
Rapids	+	2.69	10.22
	−	3.48	10.94
Pioneer x Rapids F_1	+	3.91	12.22
	−	4.25	12.66
Eureka 290	+	4.91	13.46
	−	4.30	13.16
Mean	+	3.75	11.27
	−	3.65	11.56

normal growth at somewhat higher temperatures. As there is little,
if any, ventilation of greenhouses in northern latitudes in wintertime, little carbon dioxide is lost to the outside atmosphere. Only
small quantities of carbon dioxide are required. Finally, root growth
is preferentially stimulated as compared to top growth which aids in
a rapid recovery following transplanting.

◎ *Nutrient Levels and Fertilizers.* Soil or artificial soil mixes
used for starting plants and in greenhouse beds should either be
sterile or be sterilized, preferably with steam, or fumigated well in
advance of using. The pH should range between 6.2 and 7.0, and the
growing medium should be low in soluble salts.

An excellent fertilizer for promoting early plant growth is a
50-50 mixture, by weight, of di-ammonium and mono-potassium
phosphates. Di-ammonium phosphate is sufficient for some western
soils and some artificial media. All fertilizers applied during plant

Figure 23. *Carbon dioxide enrichment of greenhouse atmospheres is most valu-*
able for the production of an early spring crop of greenhouse tomatoes. The
generators here are on the outside of the greenhouses.

growth should be added to the irrigation water. Concentrations may be varied from one-fourth to one ounce per gallon, depending on plant size and the frequency of application. Fertilizers low in chlorides, sodium, and sulphates are good insurance against the accumulation of excess soluble salts.

The best results with tomato seedlings can be obtained only if soil nutrient levels are high. Container grown plants and those transplanted to ground beds should be heavily fertilized. During the dark cloudy weather of late fall and early winter, the growth of potted plants is controlled by withholding water, not mineral nutrients. High nitrogen and phosphorus levels during the early seedling stages are necessary to produce the maximum number of flowers and fruit.

In a typical experiment, as the nitrogen was increased, flower numbers were increased (Table 6). The more nitrogen the plants received, the more flowers they produced. The addition of phosphorus also increased the number of flowers in the first cluster. Cold treated plants had the most flowers at the highest level of both nitrogen and phosphorus.

Ideal tomato plants can be grown according to the following program. Spacing should be sufficiently wide to avoid overlapping of leaves by neighboring plants. Growth is controlled by withholding water. Leaves will be dark green and closely spaced, the stems thick and sturdy, and the flower buds early and well formed. If fertilizer is applied frequently, good plant growth can be maintained. This should be until the flower buds are well developed on the first cluster without undue hardening of the plants.

TABLE 6. Effects of nitrogen and phosphorus levels in the root medium on flower numbers of the first clusters of Michigan–Ohio Hybrid tomato plants that received the cold treatment.

		Nitrogen levels (ppm)			
Phosphorus levels (ppm)		Low (100)	Medium (200)	High (400)	Phosphorus level means
(flower numbers in first clusters)					
Low	(15)	9.7	8.7	14.3	10.9
Medium	(30)	7.3	9.3	15.0	10.5
High	(60)	5.3	12.3	15.3	11.0
Nitrogen level means		7.4	10.1	14.9	

Recommendations for maintaining high soil nutrient levels for young tomato plants follow:

> As seedlings emerge in seed flats or the seed bed, water them with a solution of soluble fertilizer. It should be high in phosphate with moderate levels of nitrogen and potash. Analyses of 10–52–17 or 9–45–15 have proven satisfactory. For western soils high in potassium, di-ammonium phosphate is recommended. Use ½ ounce per gallon (4 grams per liter) when watering. When the plants are pricked-off into pots or beds, water once again with the above fertilizer solution. Repeat at 5- to 10-day intervals. When the plants are small, fertilize every 7-10 days with ½ ounce per gallon of water. Two to three weeks before setting into ground beds, fertilize every 4 or 5 days with 1 ounce of fertilizer per gallon of water. This is equal to 3 pounds in 50 gallons of water which is enough for a single watering of 1500 to 2000 well developed plants.

◉   *Chemical Treatments.* Chemicals may either retard or stimulate tomato flowering. Those such as N-m-tolyphthalamic acid (Duraset–20W) applied to young seedlings during the sensitive period (ten days to two weeks following cotyledon expansion) may increase flower numbers several fold. "Auxins" generally increase flower numbers and may induce tomato plants to flower earlier. "CCC" accelerates flowering by reducing the time to the first open flower; fewer leaves are formed before the first flower cluster. Gibberellin decreases flower numbers, and elongates the styles of the flowers so that the stigma may extend beyond the stamen cones. It may promote anther development and pollen production in otherwise male sterile types. Maleic hydrazide and "phosphon" compounds also delay flowering.

There is no relationship between chemical growth promotion or inhibition in the tomato plant and flower formation. No chemical effects are as reproducible as those of temperature, light, carbon dioxide, or nutrient level. *The use of chemicals to regulate tomato flowering is not recommended.*

◉   *Combination of Factors Most Conducive to Early and Prolific Flowering.* The greenhouse tomato is one of the few horticultural plants in which flower production may limit fruit production. All plant-growing procedures should therefore be aimed toward maximum flower production as early as possible. Once flowering and fruit production are initiated, the effects of temperature, light, carbon dioxide, and nutrient levels are multiplied; and the memory seems to be transmitted to later flower clusters. Cultural practices and environmental regulations then become more simplified.

The ideal combination would be as follows. During the ten days to three weeks following cotyledon expansion, temperatures both in the air and root zone should be maintained in the mid-fifties. Natural day lengths in mid-winter and early spring should not be extended by artificial lights, but artificial lights can be used to supplement natural light intensity. Cool white or wide-spectrum fluorescent lights are superior to incandescent tungsten filament bulbs. The metal halide and high pressure sodium vapor lamps are even more efficient. High nutrient levels, particularly nitrogen and phosphorus, should be maintained in the root media. Growth should be regulated by controlling soil moisture, not by restricting fertilizer applications. Carbon dioxide levels of 1000 to 1200 ppm should be provided in the greenhouse atmosphere during the daylight hours. Finally, the grower should select varieties which have a desirable flowering behavior and which respond significantly to the above modifications in the environment.

◉ *Pre-Transplant Handling of Plants and Transplanting into Ground Beds.* Every means should be employed for maximum utilization of the available sunlight for flower formation. The cold treatment should be followed by night temperatures no higher than 58 to 62°F. Day temperatures should not exceed 65 to 75°F on sunny or partly cloudy days, and 60 to 65°F on cloudy days (Table 1). Plants should be held as dry as possible without wilting, and fertility levels kept high by periodic watering with soluble fertilizers high in phosphate.

Good growth without excessive elongation should be maintained. At no time is excessive hardening recommended and seeding should be delayed so that it will not be necessary. *The width of the young plants should at all times be equal to or even greater than the height* (Fig. 24). The cotyledons should be large, the stem thick, and the leaves dark green and closely spaced. Strong side shoots will develop. When the leaves of potted or bed grown plants begin to touch, they should be spaced progressively farther apart. This is

Figure 24. *The width of potted plants should at all times be equal to or even greater than the height, the stems thick, the leaves dark green and spaced close together. Flower buds should also be prominent as on the plant on the right at the time of transplanting into ground beds.*

especially important during the two or three weeks prior to transplanting into the ground beds.

Plants should be transplanted when the first flower buds become prominent, a week to ten days before the buds open (Fig. 24, right). If high fertility levels are maintained and watering and spacing are carefully controlled, plants may be held until they flower. During the late fall and winter, this will be fifty-five to sixty-five days after seeding. At no time should nutrients be withheld to suppress growth.

◉ *Custom Plant Growing.* Use of custom grown plants is on the increase in the United States and is moving abroad. Plants are sold either in individual containers such as peat pots or soil blocks, or as rooted plants. When low greenhouse temperatures are used for crops of winter lettuce, growers may find it more economical to purchase plants, than raising the temperature in portions of the greenhouse to grow their own. Modified growth chambers for tomato plant production have been created from discarded cold storage units by installing artificial lights. Plant growing boxes may be constructed by the use of 4' x 8' plywood with the edges turned up which gives a dimension of 3' x 7' and 6" deep (Fig. 15).

Seeds are sown directly in soil boxes and maintained under controlled environments until the plants are sold; or they may be transplanted into other containers or soil beds. The seeds are sown singly for both methods. The spacing for the former is greater than for those to be transplanted. Space sown seeds make transplanting easier and more efficient than the cluster sown. The roots are easily separated at transplanting without damage.

Sowing seeds singly is achieved by means of a seeding board with holes spaced evenly and provided with suction through each nozzle so that one seed is held at each hole. The board is placed on the germinating medium and suction released so that a pin slides from each nozzle pushing the seed on the medium which is later covered, firmed, and watered. Other seeding boards have holes with suction that holds the seeds and flushes the seed by a quick jet of air when the board is placed on the medium.

Following seeding, the plant boxes are placed in a thermostatically controlled 70-75°F degree chamber without lights until the seedlings emerge. They are then moved to a lighted chamber with a 12 hour light cycle until the first true leaves emerge. The plants may then be moved to a greenhouse or held in the growth chambers. The germinating medium in the boxes is made either of a peat-vermiculite or sand-peat mixes. Soil used in peat pots is either peat-vermiculite or a standard greenhouse mix. Peat-vermiculite, sand-peat, or sandy loam soil have been used successfully when plants are grown in beds or boxes and sold as rooted plants. In the north where winter light is limited, supplementary light such as provided by metal halide or high pressure sodium vapor lamps is being used to grow seedlings and transplants.

◉ *Fertilization and Steam Sterilization of Ground Beds Before Transplanting.* Soils used for greenhouse tomato production should be high in organic matter. This may be accomplished by an annual application of the equivalent of one hundred yards (tons) of manure per acre. There are problems, however, in using manure. Excessive nitrogen may be released during decomposition, and large amounts of ammonium nitrogen are produced following steam sterilization.

If manure is not available or if soluble salts are high, growers should work large quantities of organic matter into the soil from the mulches used on the previous crop. An annual application of one thousand or two thousand pounds of a commercial fertilizer such as 0–20–20 or 0–20–0 (superphosphate) is usually needed, except on heavy soils which have been cropped and fertilized for many years. One thousand pounds per acre or less is usually adequate for soils in old greenhouses, while two thousand pounds per acre may be desirable in new greenhouses.

Most growers in the Grand Rapids, Michigan area have benefited from an annual application of one hundred to two hundred pounds of manganese sulphate per acre. This is especially true where the soil pH is 6.8 or above. Manganese is not recommended in most parts of Ohio and Canada because of toxicity problems following steam sterilization. All of the above fertilizers should be tilled into the soil before transplanting the crop. Fertilizers should be applied in accordance with needs as revealed by soil tests (Tables 17, 18, 19).

Soil sterilization is important in the obtaining of high tomato yields. It is one practice the grower should not omit, since there is the possibility of losing the crop from nematodes or other soil borne diseases. Soil disinfestation agents can be either chemical or heat. Chemical disinfestants are more specific, while heat can be relied upon to destroy all pathogenic fungi, virus, bacteria, nematodes, and insects. Steam sterilization is more effective than any chemical thus far formulated. Although steam sterilization will kill the nitrifying bacteria in the soil, the use of nitrate forms of commercial fertilizer will prevent nitrogen deficiencies. The grower does not need to be alarmed about killing the nitrifying bacteria, since they will quickly repopulate.

Soil disinfestants such as Vorlex, chloropicrin, methyl bromide, Vapam, and other chemicals are used to control certain soil borne fungus diseases, nematodes, and weed seeds. Effectiveness of soil fumigants is dependent upon time and concentration of the chemicals used. The fumes of the chemicals are toxic, and caution should be taken when using them. Chemicals should be applied according to the manufacturer's recommendation. Soil temperatures should generally be high (60 to 70°F). Fumigation at temperatures below 60° is not conducive for some fumigants to volatilize rapidly enough to kill the harmful organisms. Conversely, high soil temperatures will accelerate volatilization and not hold the effective killing concentration in the soil long enough.

One of the disadvantages in the use of chemical disinfestants is that the normal dosage of chemical does not penetrate the non-decomposed root that may be infested with nematodes. Nematodes within the root are thus protected from the chemical. To obtain best results, tomato roots should be kept moist three to four weeks prior to application of the chemical. This will encourage decomposition of the infected roots.

Chemical fumigation injury is common. Do not plant for at least two weeks after fumigating, longer if the soil temperature is below 60°F. Fumigation injury may result if all of the gas does not escape prior to planting. Permanently installed clay tile lines often act as absorbents of these chemicals.

Growers may check for the presence of harmful fumigant residue by placing some of the soil in a quart jar and planting lettuce seed. After sprinkling lightly with water, the lid is placed on so that the jar is air tight. If the seed germinates, the fumigant is out of the soil. It is then safe for tomato transplants. However, if the fumigant is still present, light tillage (above the zone of fumigation) will hasten the evaporation of the chemical.

While chemical soil treatments are helpful, annual steam sterilization of the soil is necessary to sustain continuous high production of greenhouse tomatoes (Fig. 25). An increasing number of constraints are also being imposed on chemical soil fumigants. Their continued use will likely be curtailed. Steam sterilization should be from permanently installed underground tile, or their equivalent. Steaming of the soil should be thorough and of sufficient duration and depth to kill all weed seeds, insects, nematodes, and disease organisms. Serious losses from *Verticillium*, *Fusarium* and bacterial wilts, and mosaic virus can be avoided by proper sterilization of the soil before planting. Soil steaming should follow the addition of manure, and precede planting by at least six weeks to allow the soil to cool and dry. Toxic levels of ammonia and manganese formed from heating the soil can also escape, be broken down, or leached.

Soil in the ground beds at the time of transplanting should be dry or only slightly moist. The soil temperature should also be close to the desired air temperature.

⊛ *Installation of Tile.* Tiling of a greenhouse soil bed for steam sterilization may be done as follows. Trenches fourteen to fifteen inches deep and six to eight inches wide are dug, either by hand or by special trenching or tiling machines. The tile are then placed end

Figure 25. *Annual steam sterilization of the soil is necessary to sustain continuous high production. Temperatures of the soil should be maintained at 180°F or higher for 1 to 4 hours.*

to end in the trench so that the surface of the tile will be covered by approximately ten inches of soil. Use either perforated or non-perforated four-inch (diameter) tile. Down spouting of perforated tile will allow greater penetration of the steam. The tile should be in rows eighteen to twenty-four inches apart lengthwise of the beds, and laid with the perforation on the bottom or the sides. The beds should be in units which are fifty to one hundred and twenty-five feet long for sterilizing at a given time. Headers every fifty feet are recommended for rapid sterilization. In other words, the distance from center to center of the rows should be an average of eighteen to twenty-four inches, and beds should be sterilized in lengths of fifty to one hundred and twenty-five feet at a time. Thus, a house twenty feet wide would require ten to fourteen rows of tile. A few three-inch tile make effective slip joints for the four-inch tile.

Adjacent rows of tile may be looped together at the ends with properly placed elbows. If the ends of adjacent rows are thus connected, the steaming effect from the two lines will tend to be equalized. The tile should be covered with one-inch size gravel poured so that it fills in along the sides of the tile and covers the tile by one inch. The tile should be set at such a depth that they will not be broken by rototilling equipment or by other cultural practices.

Steam is introduced into the rows of tile through one of the risers of a two-inch header pipe. This header, with a twenty-inch capped riser on each end, extends across the width of the house, and is equipped with nipples one-inch in diameter and about ten inches long. One nipple corresponds with, and is cemented into, each row of tile.

Any type of soil can be effectively sterilized by steaming through tile. For effective steam sterilization, all soil within beds or benches should be held at a temperature of 180°F for one to four hours. Four hours is necessary to kill all disease-causing organisms in plant debris. This usually requires six to eight hours of steaming the soil in a particular area, but may be accomplished in three hours. Recurring pockets of disease indicate poor sterilization. Steam sterilization may be effective at either low (15 to 20 psi) or high (40 to 50 psi) pressures. The amount of tiled soil that can be steamed at any one time is approximately ten square feet per boiler horsepower. In other words, with a one hundred horsepower boiler, one thousand square feet could be effectively steamed at one time. Boilers which have been permanently installed as part of a central heating system are the usual source of steam. Portable steam generators, however, are extensively used in western Europe and on the Isle of Guernsey. They have also found limited acceptance in some of the western states in the United States.

Some growers with long experience in soil sterilization check the end of each steam tile line to be sure there is no plugging during the steaming process. A shovel is inserted into the ground directly above the steam tile, moved back and forth a few times, and then pulled out of the soil. If steam flows from this opening, then the tile line is open and functional. Growers who do a thorough job of steam sterilization may not completely rid the soil of tobacco mosaic virus and other pathogens, but will seldom have disease problems early in the growth of the crop that follows.

An alternative method for steam sterilization through permanently installed tile is with the inverted pan. The depth of heat penetration, however, is so shallow that it is recommended only for bench sterilization. The steam rake or comb is used in western Europe and to a limited extent in the United States. The steam plow is most effective after the soil is well tilled. A rake of steam pipes spaced twelve inches apart is pulled by a set of winches at the end of the greenhouse. The plow moves at the rate of about one foot per minute and drops a canvas cover behind. The steam comb consists of a set of 1¼″ pipes 12 to 15 inches long, set 12 inches apart with ⅛″ holes on the side. The comb is placed in the tilled soil and moved across the area to be sterilized.

Greenhouse soils are most appropriately sterilized during August or early September after the spring tomato crop has been removed and before the first fall lettuce or tomato crop is set. Steam sterilization, particularly oversteaming, often releases toxic amounts of ammonium and manganese. Water leaching may be necessary to remove excesses of these substances, as well as soluble salts, and to cool the soil following steam sterilization. Planting may be possible within a few days after steaming if the soil is thoroughly cooled and leached before setting the plants.

Some growers steam sterilize their greenhouse soils and then add well-rotted manure after sterilization. This may reduce the release of ammonia and other toxic substances. It also re-inoculates the soil with beneficial organisms. There is the danger, however, of re-inoculating with disease organisms as well as with weed seeds.

Successful tomato growers in Denmark and in most European countries sterilize not only the growing medium, but also the inside of the greenhouse between crops. Live steam is injected into the house until thoroughly saturated followed by injecting into the steam 6–7 pints of formalin per 1,000 square feet. The greenhouse is closed for a day and vented prior to planting of the new crop. This practice reduces the insect and disease incidence in the greenhouse.

‌ CULTURE AND MANAGEMENT OF A GREENHOUSE TOMATO CROP

Spacing and Plants Per Acre. There is no agreement among growers as to the most desirable distance between rows or between plants in the row. Optimum space per plant has been found to be between 3½ and 4½ square feet. Spacing between rows and between plants in the row should be made so that all of the greenhouse space is efficiently used without crowding which tends to favor leaf diseases and produce smaller fruits. Many growers have alternated wide and narrow rows and use the wide rows to work around the plants.

For example, if the rows are alternated between 32 and 40 inches, the average row spacing will be 36 inches and would require approximately 18 inches between plants to obtain the assumed ideal of 4½ square feet per plant. For proper air movement through the plant foliage and good light penetration to the lower leaves, the narrow rows are suggested to be not closer than 32 inches. Usually, eighty-five hundred to nine thousand plants per acre are used for fall and early spring plantings. Late spring plantings vary from ninety-three hundred to twelve thousand plants per acre. Excellent results have been obtained by spacing plants fifteen inches apart in forty-two inch rows. This spacing will give approximately ten thousand plants per acre.

The use of a wide-paned glass is highly recommended where new greenhouse units are to be constructed or old ones reconditioned. Glass sash twenty or more inches wide greatly increases the amount of sunlight transmitted into greenhouses. More plants per acre can, thus, be planted and yields increased accordingly. Glass that is more than twenty inches wide, however, is not recommended for areas of heavy snowfall or for wide houses (exceeding forty-five to fifty feet). Structures strong enough to support wind and snow loads, as well as the weight of tomato vines and fruit, are needed.

⊛ *Watering the Transplant.* If a watering solution is used at transplanting, the usual one ounce per gallon of an all-soluble fertilizer high in phosphate is added. Plants started in winter or early spring should then be spot watered as needed for several weeks after transplanting. Once established, they should go for several weeks without a general irrigation.

Mid-winter plantings at Michigan State University on a heavy loam soil are not given a general irrigation until eight to ten weeks after transplanting. The percentages of available soil moisture during this period range from ten to twenty percent at a depth of six inches. Twelve inches below the soil surface, the percentage of available moisture is from thirty to sixty percent. No general irrigation program is started until moisture levels are below twenty percent in the first twelve inches of soil. The intent is to induce deep rooting.

An acceptable irrigating and fertilizing practice for soil cultures has been proven for experimental plantings, and is now being adopted by some commercial growers. Each row of plants is set in a depression or furrow about four inches deep and ten inches wide.

Perforated black plastic hoses or "Drip Hose"[10] or a twin wall hose system laid along the plant row greatly expedite watering and reduce the labor requirement. Other more automated drip or trickle systems have also been designed. Throughout the season, all irrigation water and soluble fertilizer is added in the furrow along the plant rows. In this system only the soil in the depression along the plant row is watered. The surface soil between the rows is heavily mulched with straw and always remains dry.

⊛ *Drip Irrigation.* Trickle or drip irrigation systems had their origin 25 years ago in the production of greenhouse tomatoes in northwestern Europe. It was the first type of mechanical irrigation to be installed on any scale for greenhouse tomatoes. This automated system of water management, with its many modifications, is now used extensively in the U.S.A. and abroad. Its use has extended to many crops grown in the field. Drip irrigation is the slow release of water near the base of tomato plants in the form of drops through

[10] Chapin Watermatics, Inc., 368 N. Colorado Avenue, Watertown, New York 13601.

Figure 26. *Drip irrigation provides a slow release of water at the base of tomato plants through mechanical devices known as emitters.* (COPENHAGEN, DENMARK).

Figure 27. *Drip irrigation being used for tomato plants grown in peat modules.* (LITTLEHAMPTON, SUUSSEX, ENGLAND).

Figure 28. *Drip irrigation provided for tomato plants set in peat pots on rock wool mats.* (COPENHAGEN, DENMARK).

mechanical devices called emitters (Fig. 26). This irrigation system may be used for ordinary soil culture—with or without mulching—sand culture, peat culture, peat modules (Fig. 27), strawbale culture, rockwool culture (Fig. 28), sawdust culture or in growing young plants.

The advantages are many. The drip irrigation system puts the water where the plants are. The root medium only, rather than the soil, is irrigated. Yields of tomatoes may be increased. The water requirement is reduced. Many disease problems are alleviated because leaf and stem surfaces are kept drier. The spread of disease is kept to a minimum. Regular cultural and harvest operations may proceed without interruption. There is a substantial saving in labor. Fertilizers can be applied more efficiently. Finally, there is the ultimate in water and fertilizer management. The plants can be provided the right amount of water and nutrients at all times with no puddling or splashing. This gentle method of water application preserves soil structure and allows better soil aeration and water penetration.

Serious consideration should be given to the installation of drip irrigation in all new greenhouses. Similarly, as presently installed water management systems become non-functional, strong consideration should be given to installing a drip irrigation system.

Many types of trickle or drip emitters and systems are available. Rigid polyvinyl chloride pipe, $3/4$ to 1 inch in size, is commonly used for headers. Polyethylene pipe, $1/2$ inch in diameter, is normally used for emitter laterals because it is flexible and easy to handle. There are many kinds of drip irrigation emitters—both low and high pressure. Drip irrigation systems should be so designed that emitters are spaced about 3 feet apart. Each emitter should deliver 1 to $1 1/2$ gallons of water per hour. The amount of water that enters a drip irrigation system should be regulated by a flow control valve. Water must be filtered before flowing into a drip irrigation system. Sand, soil, plant nutrients, or any foreign substances which may cause plugging must be filtered from the water. Careful water filtration is the key to successful drip irrigation. Completely soluble fertilizers, especially nitrogen, can be applied through a drip irrigation system. Drip irrigation systems can be completely automated, with continuous monitoring of soil moisture. Costs of installation can be recovered quickly through reduced water requirements, reduced labor, higher yields, and improved fruit quality. Between crops headers and lateral lines may be tied overhead to the green-house structure. This allows tillage, fumigation, and transplanting to proceed without restriction.

⊛ *Pruning and Training.* Prior to the handling of plants, hands should be washed with soap or dipped in a mild disinfectant to reduce the spread of virus diseases. A pan of disinfectant and paper towel is placed at the entrance to the growing area.

Plants are usually trained to a single stem. All side shoots should be removed at least weekly. The use of plastic twine (Fig. 29) has eliminated the hazards formerly associated with the chemical treatment of binder or baler twines. One end of the twine is tied with a small non-slip loop to the base of the plant. The other is attached to a wire supported 6 to 8 feet above the plant row (Fig. 30). Where the practice calls for dropping or lowering of the plants, two to three feet of additional length of twine is left on when the initial

Figure 29. *The use of plastic twine has eliminated many hazards formerly associated with the chemical treatment of binder or baler twine.* (NOTE ALSO THE PEANUT HULL MULCH).

Figure 30. *Tying of plastic twine attaching a non-slip loop to the base of the plant with the other end to a wire 6–8 feet above the plant row.*

tying to the overhead wire is made. As the plant grows, it is twisted around the string in one or two easy spirals for each fruit cluster (Fig. 31). Plants from the early spring crop normally reach the overhead wire long before the season is over. The common practice, if the extra length of twine was not left at the initial tying, is to allow

Figure 31. *Training the tomato plant by twisting it around the twine, using 1 to 2 easy spirals for each fruit cluster.*

the plant to grow on the wire by tying it or allowing the growth to loop over to the next row. Where an additional portion of twine was allowed, the slip knot is removed and the plant dropped 2 to 3 feet. The lower leaves are normally removed prior to lowering the plant so that only the stem comes in contact with soil or mulch (Fig. 32).

Several training systems to extend the main stem cropping of

Figure 32. *The lower leaves are removed prior to dropping the plants so that only the stems come in contact with the soil, mulch, or rack.*

greenhouse tomatoes are practiced in Europe and in the U.S. In parts of England the main stem is topped at the overhead wire and side shoots are allowed to develop to extend the crop. Other systems are the Dutch hook, coat hanger hook, S-hook, and the Sorensen.

The Dutch hook system requires the training of the main stem to within 12 inches of the overhead wire. The stem is allowed to extend 12 to 18 inches beyond the wire. The stem is then arched over into the next hook and brought down on the twine and turned upward on its original twine approximately 3 feet from the ground.

In the coat hanger system, a modified hook with a coat hanger-shaped bobbin with the season's length of twine wound on it is unwound and the coat hanger rehooked on the overhead wire as the plants are layered.

The S-hook system requires hooks to be crimped on the overhead wire at the spacing used for tomato growing (Fig. 33). The twine for each of the plants is cut to the length required for the growing of the crop. One end of the twine is tied to the plant and the twine is passed over the hook 2 or more places away from the plant so that it is inclined and tied to the overhead wire. As the plants reaches the wire, the twine is unhooked so that the twine rests on the next hook. The use of bottom wires which provide a rack 20 inches above the ground has been recommended to rest successive clusters on each layering to prevent fruits from touching the ground. A modified rack technique is widely practiced in Denmark (Fig. 34).

A recent modification of the standard hanging method is the Sorensen system. This system, developed by G. B. Sorensen of Essex, England, involves the training of the plants to the overhead wire and the removal of the lower leaves approximately 30 inches from the ground. The twines of the first three plants in the row are cut ap-

Figure 33. *The S-hook system of attaching twine to overhead wires for training tomato plants.*

Figure 34. *The modified rack system of training tomato plants in Denmark keeps both the stems and the fruit from touching the ground.*

proximately 3 feet from the ground. The plants are then let down on the alley or path. The fourth twine is then cut at the same height and the plant is retied to twine number 1 using a simple loop tie approximately 18–24 inches from the top and the plant is twisted around the twine. The fifth plant is tied to the second twine, etc. The process continues and goes around the corner to the next row to the end and the three vacant twines at the end of the row are tied to the plants that were let down on the path in the first row.

A continuous-string method for supporting tomato plants using overhead hooks was developed by the University of Arizona Environmental Research Laboratory. The operator standing on the ground utilizes a $\frac{1}{4}$ to $\frac{1}{2}$ inch diameter, 4–5 feet hollow tube with a continuous string that passes through, places the string over the hooks and around the plant. The twine or string is fastened to the first plant with a non-slip knot, brought up and placed over 2 overhead hooks and down to the second plant, looped below the first leaf and continued to the next plant, looped below the first leaf and up to the next two hooks, etc. At the end of the row the twine is cut and tied. This method has been reported to save approximately 66 percent of the labor of the present tying methods once the hooks are initially installed on the overhead wires. Other advantages are the elimination of individual operations, the need for moving platforms used in tying the twine to the overhead wire and the simplification in removing the twine when the plants are removed.

Plastic clips[11] have been introduced (Fig. 35). They may be used as an alternative to the usual twisting method of attaching the plants to the twine. The clip is snapped together by placing the hinge area on the supporting twine and the loop position around the plant. The advantages in using the clips are a reduction in plant breakage if inexperienced help is used and the elimination of the bottom knot of twine around the base of the plant. Using plastic clips to eliminate the bottom knot may present a localized high humidity problem and poor air circulation around the lower part of the plant and the area enclosed by the clips may become a site for *Botrytis* and *Sclerotinia* stem rots.

The growing tip of tomato plants should be pruned approximately 45 days for the spring crop and 55 to 60 days for the fall crop prior to the end of the harvest period. At least 2–3 leaves should remain above the top cluster that is in bloom. Fruit clusters should be trained beneath the leaves to protect against sunscald and cracking.

Since air movement near the ground level is important as plants become taller, leaves below the ripening fruit clusters should be removed to allow for better air circulation. The leaves in this area do not receive sufficient sunlight for photosynthesis and do not contribute to fruit production. It is also suggested that while pruning or working around the plants, newly set deformed fruits should be removed. The plant resources can then be directed to the production of well formed fruit.

⊛ *Pollination.* High yields of greenhouse tomatoes can be produced only if the flowers set fruit. The first flower clusters on each

[11] Trade name—Stem-Gems. Available from Famco, Inc., 300 Lake Road, Medina, Ohio 44256.

Figure 35. *Plastic bands or clips aid in tying and training of greenhouse tomatoes.*

plant should be vibrated daily or at a minimum of every other day with an electrically or battery operated vibrator (Fig. 36). [12,13,14]

Temperature plays an important role in the shedding of pollen. Temperatures below 65°F tend to delay it while best results occur above 70°F. The temperatures in excess of 90°F often encountered in May and June for spring crops and in August and September for fall crops result in poor fruit set. The problem can be alleviated by using shading compounds on the glass or plastic, or by periodically wetting the plants through misting or overhead irrigation (Fig. 37). The resultant evaporative cooling will lower the temperatures within a greenhouse several degrees below that of the outside air.

[12] Invented by R. Zinn, 25 West Schaaf Road, Cleveland 31, Ohio. Available from Stanley Pollinator Company, 25 Schaaf Road, Cleveland, Ohio, 44131.
[13] Electric Bee Pollinator (6-volt battery). Plant Products Company, Ltd., 314 Orenda Road, Bramalea, Ontario, Canada.
[14] Dao Corporation, P.O. Box 659, Terre Haute, Ind. 47808.

Figure 36. *The electrically operated hand pollinator. Individual flower clusters are vibrated daily.*

To prevent leaf diseases, this wetting should be terminated early enough in the afternoon to allow the plant surfaces to dry by evening.

Pollen is shed most abundantly on bright sunny days between 10 a.m. and 4 p.m. Wind machines, air jets, water jets, and other gadgets, including the ultrasonic whistle, have not proven completely satisfactory for pollination in the northern states. Air jets are used successfully in the southwestern parts of the U.S.A., and water jets in Britain (Fig. 38). Tapping or mechanical jarring of the wires is effective only if sunlight and temperatures are adequate, pollen is shedding, and fruit clusters are three to four feet above the ground.

Recently, automatic pollination systems using an electric-pneumatic system which regulates the vibration of wires have been reported fairly successful. The short bursts, strokes, and speed are adjustable. This system is valuable when labor is not available for pollination. The cost of the system is estimated at $3,000–5,000 per acre.

There is a great need for further innovation and mechanization of the pollination of greenhouse tomatoes. This operation now constitutes a significant and costly labor expenditure in greenhouse tomato production. Total mechanization and automatic control of

Figure 37. *Overhead sprinkle irrigation of greenhouse tomatoes. This method of irrigation has the advantage of evaporative cooling during hot weather.*

pollination are still to be sought after. If coupled with environmental control, variety selection, and cultural programs, hand pollination may be eventually eliminated.

Regular vibrating for pollination, pruning, and training are necessary in greenhouse tomato production. These practices, however, often result in the rapid transmission of mosaic virus diseases from infected to healthy plants. When infected plants are discovered, they should be handled only after healthy plants have been cared for. Separate equipment should also be used.

◉ *Fruit Setting.* Tomato production depends upon flower formation and fruit set. Poor fruit setting on apparently healthy tomato plants depends upon the climatic conditions prior to and at the time of pollination. Low light intensities, short photoperiods, and high night temperatures may all be important limiting factors. The most common symptom is that the flowers abscise at or shortly after anthesis. It is commonly called blossom drop or truss abortion.

There are numerous reasons for failures in fruit set: (1) sudden cold or cool temperatures when plants are in bloom, (2) hot dry weather, especially drying winds, (3) injury by thrips, (4) lack of moisture, and (5) extensive vine growth.

Research has shown that low temperatures after pollination do not reduce fruit set. Low temperatures do not inhibit pollen shedding or pollination. Although low temperatures did not affect fruit set of open flowers, they did cause poor fruit set of flowers that opened 2 weeks after the cold period. Flowers pollinated during the unfruitful period had very little pollen and the pollen was highly sterile. When the same plants, however, were pollinated with pollen from plants grown in previously warmer temperatures, they were fertile. This suggests that low temperatures reduce fruit set of tomatoes through an influence on gametogenesis and especially on pollen formation. With plants grown at 50–55°F, the flowers produced little or no pollen, meiosis was relatively normal in the pollen mother cell, but the degeneration of pollen usually occurred prior to anthesis. Pollen produced at low temperature had low viability.

Figure 38. *A water stream jet is effective for aiding in the pollination of tomato flowers in England.*

High temperatures, low humidity, and low moisture increase blossom drop. During periods of high temperature and low humidity the flower style elongates prior to dehiscence. This condition results in failure of pollination because the stigma may extend beyond the stamen cone and there is a destruction of the stigmatic surface before pollination can be effected. The flowers, therefore, fail to become fertilized and soon abscise.

Flower development is also dependent upon soil moisture and temperature. Apparently, the temperature 3 days prior to anthesis has the greatest influence. Even without style elongation at high temperatures, fruit set is often very low. This suggests that pollen germination and tube growth may be retarded at high temperatures.

Temperatures have a marked effect on the germination percentage of pollen, as well as on the rate of tube growth. Germination of pollen was higher at 85°F than at 70° over a period of 60 hours. Germination at 50°F was 20 percent, while at 100°F it was only 6 percent.

The maximum rate of pollen-tube growth occurred at 70°F, and decreased in descending order at 85, 50 and 100°F. Pollen is inactive for several hours after pollination and before germination. Fertilization was first observed 50 hours after pollination. Initiation of growth of embryo and endosperm was found to occur between 82 and 94 hours, respectively, after pollination at 60–75°. Pollen tube growth was slow even at the optimum temperatures of 70–85°F. Fertilization at 100°F is unlikely before the contents of the embyrosac disintegrate at this temperature. Fruit set is abundant only when the night temperatures are between 60 and 70. With lower and higher temperatures during the night, fruiting is reduced or absent.

Use of an evaporative cooling system is suggested where the humidity of the air outside is low. Another approach is through the use of evaporative cooling of the micro-climate around the tomato plant by application of 0.04 to .06 inch of water per hour of mist irrigation or by modified sprinkling systems (Fig. 37). During high temperatures, such practices should be terminated in time to allow the leaves to dry prior to nightfall.

A saturated solution of tri-sodium phosphate for cleaning greenhouse tools, especially pollinators, is very effective in reducing the transmission of tobacco mosaic virus. Use of the solution at the end of each row helps to keep the virus isolated in infected plantings.

⊛ *Fruit Setting Chemicals.* Many chemicals sprayed onto tomato blossoms will cause the fruit to grow without pollination. At
one time fruit setting chemicals were widely used in many commercial greenhouse plantings. They still are in Japan. The practice,
however, in the U.S. was quickly discontinued and even outlawed
by some cooperative marketing groups. Indiscriminate use of chemical sprays by many growers and their failure to use good accompanying cultural practices resulted in soft, misshapen fruit of poor color
and storage quality. Chemical growth substances have been used to
an advantage where their application was restricted to the first
flower clusters. They may also be used to supplement, but not
replace, regular vibration of the flowers for pollination. The tendency has been, however, for growers who use chemical sprays to
rely on them exclusively and neglect the other practices necessary
to insure good fruit set. If chemical sprays for fruit setting are
applied to the later forming flower clusters and the fruit ripens in
hot weather, the chemically set fruit is often of inferior quality.

In view of the many hazards involved, the high probability of
impairing fruit quality, and questions of legal permissibility, *chemical sprays for improving fruit setting of greenhouse tomatoes are not
recommended.* Furthermore, all the functional flowers that a tomato
plant produces can usually be induced to set fruit by use of the
electric vibrator, and if the recommended cultural practices outlined
above are followed.

⊛ *Carbon Dioxide Enrichment.* Ninety years ago the potential
benefits of higher than normal atmospheric levels of carbon dioxide
were recognized and reported for practical greenhouse crop production in Germany, a few years later in England, and seventy years
ago in the United States. The neglect, in both Europe and America,
of the production potential of atmospheric enrichment with carbon
dioxide has been referred to as an "abandoned gold mine." The
benefits, as well as the economics of carbon dioxide enrichment of
greenhouse atmospheres, were not re-established in Europe and the
U.S. with confidence and certainty until the early 1960's.

Carbon dioxide has produced the most spectacular yield increases
of any growth factor yet discovered in the culture of greenhouse
crops. The accomplishments during the last 20 years are similar to
those which occurred a century ago when the benefits of chemical

fertilizers were first utilized in crop production. The results of carefully controlled greenhouse experiments reaffirm what the biochemist and plant physiologist have learned from studies with tank culture of algae, excised leaves, and intact plants. Under many conditions, the most limiting factor in the growth of terrestrial plants is the carbon dioxide concentration in the atmosphere. This is particularly true for greenhouse crops, since the carbon dioxide level in the enclosed atmosphere is often depleted far below that of the 330 ppm in the outside air.

The now widespread use of carbon dioxide enrichment in greenhouse crop culture, and as a variable in scientific studies in greenhouse and growth chambers, is attributed to an unusual set of circumstances which have developed almost simultaneously during the past twenty years. First, remarkable increases in yield, improved quality, and accelerated maturity in all flower and vegetable crops have been demonstrated. Second, safe and economical combustion units which utilize natural gas or fuel oils of low sulfur content are now available. Third, the development of combustion units was preceded by the use of relatively pure forms of carbon dioxide—dry ice, cylinder carbon dioxide, or low pressure liquid sources. Fourth, the economic returns exceed by severalfold the costs of treatment. Fifth, carbon dioxide monitoring and measuring devices of simple design have been developed at reasonable cost. Sixth, modern advancements in plastics have provided perforated tubing for distribution and circulation of the generated gas. Finally, there have been remarkable advancements in production technology, as well as a more thorough understanding of the factors (light, temperature, moisture, soil nutrients, diseases, insects) that affect growth.

The results with greenhouse-grown tomatoes have been phenomenal. They may be delineated as follows. Since growth rates are accelerated, the fruit matures earlier. The production peak is shifted forward (Table 7). There is an increase in both fruit setting and fruit size in spring tomato crops (Table 8); the primary effect on fall crops is larger fruit (Table 9). The Michigan results have generally been confirmed by those in Ohio (Table 10).

The carbon dioxide response is genetically dependent. Varietal differences have been noted with every crop thus far evaluated.

The increases in fruit yields range from ten to seventy percent, with averages of from fifteen to fifty-five percent (Fig. 39).

The response to carbon dioxide occurs over a wide range of light

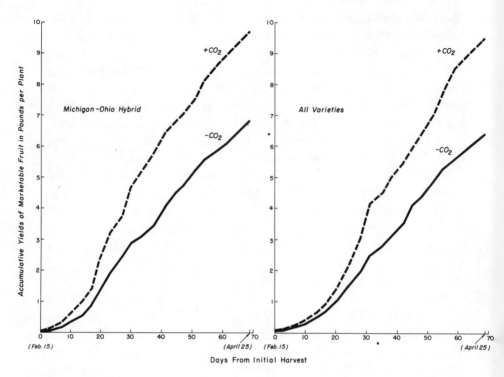

Figure 39. *Effects of carbon dioxide enrichment on the accumulative yields of greenhouse tomatoes.*

intensities. It is possible to compensate partially for low light intensities such as occur on cloudy wintry days by adding carbon dioxide to the atmosphere.

Young plants have a higher optimal requirement for carbon dioxide than old plants. This may be related to other growth factors which become progressively more limiting as plants age.

Carbon dioxide levels in non-ventilated greenhouses are generally lowest in mid-winter on bright sunny days from about 10 a.m. to 4 p.m. because of the heavy demands and removal resulting from high rates of photosynthesis. During this period, supplemental carbon dioxide is most beneficial for increasing yields of greenhouse tomatoes. To get the maximum benefit from carbon dioxide enrichment, keep the ventilators closed as much and as long as possible. The use of double layer plastic over glass greenhouses to conserve heat in midwinter may also greatly restrict air exchange. Under these conditions a supplementary source of carbon dioxide during

TABLE 7. Comparative harvest patterns, yields, and fruit size of a commercial planting of glasshouse tomatoes, with and without supplemental carbon dioxide (Spring crop, 1964, variety WR–7).[a]

| | Percent of total crop harvested by months | |
Month of Harvest	Control	Supplementary CO_2 (1500 ppm)
March	0	2
April	11	21
May	35	30
June	40	33
July	14	14
Total yield (lbs./plant)	14.5	18.4
Fruit size in oz.	5.4	6.4
Increase in yield from CO_2	——	27%
Increase in fruit size from CO_2	——	19%

[a] In cooperation with Ellis D. Hoag, Elyria, Ohio 44035.

TABLE 8. Effects of carbon dioxide on yield and fruit size of several greenhouse tomato varieties grown as early and late spring crops (East Lansing, Michigan).

| | Concentration of carbon dioxide (ppm) | | |
Variety	300	1000	Increase
	(Lbs. marketable fruit/plant)		(%)
A. *Early spring crop* (Feb. 15–June 1, 1963)			
Michigan–Ohio Hybrid–3	9.6	13.6	42
WR–7	9.3	15.9	71
WR–25	8.4	13.3	58
Spartan Red 8	7.5	11.8	57
Tuckcross 0	12.2	15.7	29
Mean (20 varieties)	9.8	14.0	43
Mean fruit size (oz.)	4.0	4.5	13
B. *Late spring crop* (May 1–July 25, 1965)			
Michigan–Ohio Hybrid–3	12.2	13.8	13
WR–7	10.8	14.6	43
Spartan Red 8	10.1	14.3	43
Michiana 138	14.3	15.2	6
Mean (17 varieties)	11.4	13.5	18
Mean fruit size (oz.)	4.9	5.4	10

daylight hours must be provided to assure optimal growth and productivity.

The optimal concentration appears to be 1,000 to 1,200 ppm. This, however, may be a limitation established by the abundance or lack of other growth factors, notably light, mineral nutrients, temperature, or moisture.

Elevated levels of atmospheric carbon dioxide promote side shoot development, longer and thicker internodes, heavier root growth, more intense pigmentation of the foliage, and earlier senescence of older leaves.

The highest yield increases from any growth factor beginning with a generally acceptable performance level have been obtained with carbon dioxide enrichment.

Particularly exciting has been the observation that extra carbon dioxide substantially increases the growth and accelerates develop-

TABLE 9. Effects of carbon dioxide on yield and fruit size of several greenhouse tomato varieties grown as fall crops (East Lansing, Michigan).

Variety	Concentration of carbon dioxide (ppm)		
	300	1000	Increase
	(Lbs. marketable fruit/plant)		(%)
A. *Fall crop* (Oct. 1–Dec. 15, 1964)			
Michigan–Ohio Hybrid–3	6.0	9.1	52
WR–7	5.7	8.6	51
Michiana 138	7.3	10.0	37
Spartan Red 8	4.9	6.5	33
Tuckcross 0	7.2	9.3	29
Spartan Pink 10	5.5	8.0	45
Mean	6.1	8.6	41
Mean fruit size (oz.)	3.9	4.9	26
B. *Fall crop* (Oct. 15, 1965–Jan. 1, 1966)			
Michigan–Ohio Hybrid–3	5.3	8.5	60
WR–7	4.2	7.0	67
Michiana 138	4.2	7.5	79
Michigan–Ohio Hybrid–25	5.3	7.8	47
WR–25	5.1	7.1	40
WR–29	4.6	7.6	65
Mean	4.8	7.6	58
Mean fruit size (oz.)	3.4	5.0	47

ment of greenhouse-grown tomatoes in winter and during periods when sunlight limits growth. Conversely, the benefits of carbon dioxide can be greatly magnified if the same crops are provided with additional light.

TABLE 10. Influence of CO_2 enrichment on total yield of greenhouse tomatoes at two different day temperature ranges. Figures are averages of 216 plants of three or more cultivars. (Data courtesy of Drs. Dale W. Kretchman and Freeman S. Howlett, Ohio Agricultural Research and Development Center, Wooster, Ohio 44691.)

Crop	Year	Day temp. range °F	Status CO_2	Yield pounds/ plant	% Yield increase from CO_2
Spring	1964	69–77	added	11.70	+5.4
			normal	11.10	
		73–81	added	11.60	+7.9
			normal	10.75	
	1965	69–77	added	16.36	+18.6
			normal	13.80	
		73–81	added	15.99	+21.3
			normal	13.29	
	1966	69–77	added	17.48	+22.8
			normal	14.22	
		73–81	added	16.28	+8.5
			normal	15.01	
	1967	69–77	added	17.36	+24.3
			normal	13.96	
		73–81	added	15.85	+18.1
			normal	13.42	
Fall	1964	65–73	added	7.92	+11.4
			normal	7.11	
		69–77	added	8.68	+2.4
			normal	8.48	
	1965	65–73	added	8.74	+8.7
			normal	8.04	
		69–77	added	8.85	+7.7
			normal	8.22	
	1966	69–77	added	11.34	+12.8
			normal	9.88	
		73–81	added	10.82	+5.3
			normal	10.28	

Some recent tests have shown no significant differences in vegetative growth of tomato plants grown at 400, 800, or 1200 ppm of carbon dioxide. Neither was there a difference in the number or development of the flowers. Plants grown, however, at either 800 or 1200 ppm had both a significantly greater fruit number and greater fruit weight.

Until now, carbon dioxide has been the limiting growth factor for many otherwise well-grown greenhouse crops. Future projections suggest that other factors, particularly mineral nutrition, moisture and light, insect and disease control, will assume greater importance. Optimal results with additional carbon dioxide will not be achieved unless the other unfavorable aspects of the environment are corrected and there are no yield reductions from other competing biological systems. The results with tomatoes suggest the importance of additional nitrogen, water, and boron.

It is no longer necessary, or desirable, to design and conduct experiments to establish the effects of carbon dioxide on greenhouse-grown crops. Ample evidence is already available. Numerous experiments with carbon dioxide enriched atmospheres for greenhouse tomatoes have established the following: The optimal concentration appears to be near 1,000–1,200 ppm. Practically all investigators have settled on this level as a base for evaluating the effects of carbon dioxide. Responses to carbon dioxide, at least in many crops, are in part temperature and light independent. There is no evidence that light, even in cloudy weather, is so poor that plants cannot utilize extra carbon dioxide. Future studies with carbon dioxide need to focus on interactions of this variable with differences in temperature, light, moisture, and mineral nutrients in root media and the relative humidity of the atmosphere.

The economic returns for carbon dioxide enrichment of greenhouse atmospheres are severalfold the investment. In the first commercial usage during the early 1960's, pure carbon dioxide was supplied from cylinders, dry ice, or tanks of the low pressure liquid. Some of these are still the primary sources in western Europe. Even these relatively expensive sources give an acceptable return on the investment. A rapid transition occurred, however, in the U.S. in the mid-sixties, to combusion units of varying degrees of refinement, utilizing fuel oils, propane, or natural gas. The usual design now consists of burners either within (Fig. 40) or outside (Fig. 41) the greenhouse which may or may not have a source of outside air. An

Figure 40. *Carbon dioxide enrichment with a natural gas combustion unit inside the greenhouse. Note the fan to pick up the exhausted gases, and perforated plastic tube to circulate and distribute the discharged CO_2.* (K. DEHAAN GREENHOUSES, GRAND RAPIDS, MICHIGAN).

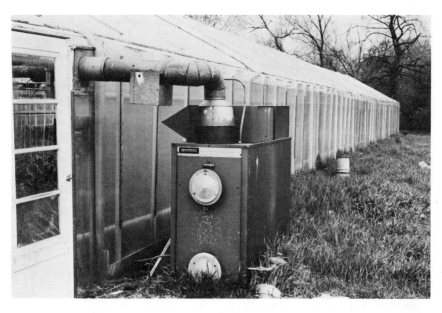

Figure 41. *A carbon dioxide combustion unit (Tectrol) placed outside a plastic greenhouse that uses outside air. The discharged CO_2 is picked up by a fan and circulated through perforated plastic tubing through the greenhouse.* (HOLWERDA BROTHERS GREENHOUSES, GRAND RAPIDS, MICHIGAN).

Figure 42. *Perforated plastic tubes facilitate the circulation and distribution of generated carbon dioxide.*

Figure 43. *A new greenhouse design for ventilation and insulation utilizing plastic and fiberglass.* (SUPERIOR FARMING COMPANY, INC., TUCSON, ARIZONA).

attached or adjacent fan to pick up the exhausted gases and transmit them through perforated plastic tubes completes the circulation and distribution of the discharged carbon dioxide (Fig. 42). In the northern states in mid-winter, these combustion units also serve as a heat source. The records of costs and returns have demonstrated an increase in yields and financial returns far beyond the costs of the carbon dioxide. The demonstrated effects of and economic returns from elevated levels of carbon dioxide suggest that all commercial greenhouse structures should be designed with the capability for carbon dioxide enrichment and its control as a variable.

Recently, the Dutch have innovated a new concept in carbon dioxide enrichment through the use of a centralized carbon dioxide generator. Most all growers have converted to the new system. Carbon dioxide is taken from flue gases of the gas heating boiler and pumped via plastic tubes into the greenhouses. The boiler flue is fitted with an automatic valve and slow running fan that extracts the gases without upsetting the draft in the flue. The gases are mixed with about two parts of air and are then pumped with a more powerful fan into the greenhouse and are distributed to individual houses through perforated plastic tubes. These tubes are placed at ground level and along the plant rows. It was noted that a boiler malfunction could give combustion gases high in carbon monoxide and ethylene. These could cause damage to the tomato crop by scorching the leaves and reduce the fruit on the clusters.

There are reports of damage to greenhouse tomato plants from carbon dioxide enrichment. Leaf desiccation and curling and vine twisting may occur. Plants with large amounts of calcium in the growing medium have shown injury. Plants with wet leaves may develop a slightly yellow and transparent spotting.

It is apparent that a total systems approach must be taken when carbon dioxide enrichment is included in greenhouse culture of tomatoes. Relevant factors include type of structure, ventilation capabilities, location, season, variety, market, economics, control systems available, and carbon dioxide source. Carbon dioxide enrichment is of potential value only when air venting is at a minimum during the day for at least a few months during the year.

◉   *Air Circulation and Ventilation.* New approaches in ventilation and insulation have paralleled the increasing use of plastics and fiberglass in greenhouse construction (Fig. 43). More and more greenhouses are being built without the conventional overhead and side ventilators. In mild weather, ventilation and cooling are provided by fans at one end and open sash or wet pads at the other. Without a closed greenhouse, however, it is impossible to get good efficiency when cooling with the fan and pad arrangement. This may occur in fiberglass houses which do not provide a closed air system.

Fall, winter, and spring often present a ventilation problem. When the air from the outside is pulled into the greenhouse at one end and exhausted at the opposite, the house may be too cold at the inlet and too warm at the fan end. Differences of 10–15°F have been noted within the same house. This often results in failures in fruit set, uneven growth, and severe foliage diseases.

Drawing air from the outside through overhead polyethylene tubes or sleeves that extend the length of the greenhouse is one solution. Holes are placed in the tubes at regular intervals and oriented horizontally so that the flow of air is across the tops of the plants. Fresh and warm air may also be introduced into a greenhouse by extending plastic tubes from the outside to overhead suspended fan type heaters.

Fresh air should periodically be taken into greenhouses at night as well as during the day, especially in plastic houses. Several feet of overhead air space above the plants should be provided to allow a good air flow through the house when the exhaust fans operate. The length of air flow should not exceed one hundred and twenty feet. Good air exchange is the best means of controlling fungus diseases affecting aerial plant parts.

Fans and turbulators have multiple values in greenhouses. Air pockets are reduced and a uniform temperature is maintained with higher temperatures at the plant level. This reduces the heat requirement, facilitates fruit setting, lowers the relative humidity and consequently the incidence of foliage diseases, especially gray mold (*Botrytis cineria*) and leaf mold (*Cladosporium fulvum*).

Studies with carbon dioxide enrichment of greenhouse atmospheres have drawn attention to at least one other important advantage of turbulators, fans, and air circulating systems. Air movement through plant foliage will reduce the gas diffusion resistance near leaf surfaces. Whether carbon dioxide enriched or not, greenhouse crops should benefit from air circulation. Turbulence maintains a higher carbon dioxide level at the leaf surface. The enclosed atmosphere of a greenhouse is an ideal environment for both adding carbon dioxide and keeping its level high at the photosynthetic site. Greenhouses should be constructed without barriers (posts, etc.) that obstruct air movement.

Forced air fan systems should be used where possible. Heating pipes (plastic or metal) between alternate rows are also ideal for promoting air movement by convection. Perforated plastic tubes or sleeves for distributing the heat from the source have proven effective. Some heat should originate along the rows at or near the ground level. Heat may be necessary late at night and during the early morning hours even if outside temperatures are mild. It is the only effective means of preventing the humid conditions within the foliage that result in the moisture condensation that encourages the spread of fungus diseases.

⊛ *Disease Control by Cultural Practices—Fungus Diseases.* Many successful operators in an effort to keep diseases out of their houses provide shoe dipping pans containing disinfectants. Visitors and workers are asked to dip the soles of their shoes prior to entering the growing area.

There are at least four serious fungus diseases that affect the foliage and, directly or indirectly, the fruit of tomatoes grown in greenhouses. In general, the problems are greater in plastic and fiberglass than in glass greenhouses. All are encouraged by high humidity. The most prevalent and serious during the late fall, winter, and early spring is gray mold (*Botrytis cineria*). This fungus thrives at low (below 65°F) temperatures and often attacks fruit on the lower clusters (Fig. 44). Leaves and particularly the stems are subject to infection at the site where plastic bands are attached (Fig. 45). Late blight (*Phytophthora infestans*) can also occur at low temperatures. Early blight (*Alternaria solani*) has a high temperature requirement. Leaf mold (*Cladosporium fulvum*) flourishes under warm (65 to 75°F), humid (above 95 percent relative humidity) conditions. It is the most destructive disease that affects greenhouse-grown tomatoes in the fall of the year. Control of these fungus diseases is a prerequisite for the successful culture of tomatoes in greenhouses. Much can be done to control all of these diseases if the suggestions outlined above and those which follow as to air circulation, ventilation, and optimal temperatures are followed.

The most serious foliage disease problems with greenhouse-

Figure 44. *Fruit infected with gray mold* (BOTRYTIS CINERIA).

Figure 45. *Sites on the stems near plastic bands often become infected with gray mold resulting from unfavorable drying conditions after watering. Note the peanut hull mulch.*

grown tomatoes occur at or near the soil level. Here, where the leaves are shaded, and they are the oldest and least resistant, air circulation is the poorest, humidity is the highest, and temperatures the lowest. Circulation can be greatly improved by removing leaves to the level of the ripening fruit (Fig. 32). All leaves are progressively removed up to the top four feet of the plant in the "nurseries" on the Isle of Guernsey. For American varieties, leaves may be removed to within five feet of the tip of the plant or up to the fruit cluster that is ripening.

A heating and air circulating system that will avoid cold air pockets and a build-up of humidity around the base of the plants should be designed. Heating lines, whether plastic tubes or metal pipes, should be placed between rows and as close to the ground as possible (Fig. 46). Growers in the United States have used ground tube heating successfully in eliminating botrytis and leaf mold. Fan and perforated plastic tubing systems or turbulators may be installed. Temperatures should seldom if ever drop below 60°F at night. Ventilator openings should be carefully regulated. During the late spring, summer, and early fall, some heat should be used at

Figure 46. *Heating lines should be placed between rows and as close to the ground as possible.* (STATE FARM MOSCOW U.S.S.R., JULY *1977*).

night, even though ventilators may be slightly open at the same time.

Although highly beneficial in other ways, mulches may be conducive to greater disease severity. They often restrict air movement near the base of plants, keep the soil cold, and may serve as carriers and harbor disease organisms. Where *Botrytis cineria* (gray mold) is severe, heavy mulches should be avoided.

Using the trench system of growing in soil will reduce high humidity problems. The rows of plants are set in a shallow depression four to six inches deep and eight to twelve inches wide. Watering is then restricted to the trench and the remainder of the ground surface is kept dry. More recently, the use of trickle or drip type of irrigation aids in reducing humidity.

⊛ *Control of Fruit Disorders by Cultural Practices—Fruit Cracking.* This disorder is usually most severe in late spring and summer in the spring crop and in early autumn for the fall crop. Cracking becomes progressively more severe as the fruit ripens. It can be alleviated by harvesting the fruit daily with the first pink color.

Temperature gradients within the fruit predispose the fruit to cracking. Avoid direct sun exposure on the fruit. Tomato plants do not require the full intensity of sunlight during late spring and early summer for maximum production. Shading compounds applied on the glass or plastic in late spring and summer reduce direct sun exposure as well as temperatures. More foliage should be allowed to develop over the fruit. Reduced trimming is recommended in late spring and early summer as the harvest time nears the end. Shading of the fruit by any means will alleviate cracking.

Marked fluctuations in moisture levels often accompanied by rapid changes in temperature result in cracking of the fruit. Organic mulches and frequent but light waterings are helpful.

Blossom-End Rot. This disorder results from withdrawal of water from the fruit by the leaves. Different degrees of the problem are illustrated in Figure 47. It may occur under any condition resulting in moisture stress; low calcium levels in the root medium are a contributing cause. Maintain adequate calcium in the root medium and avoid excess nitrogen, potassium, and other soluble salts. Again, organic mulches and frequent applications of irrigation water may be helpful. A foliage spray application of one percent calcium chloride will often give immediately beneficial results. This is

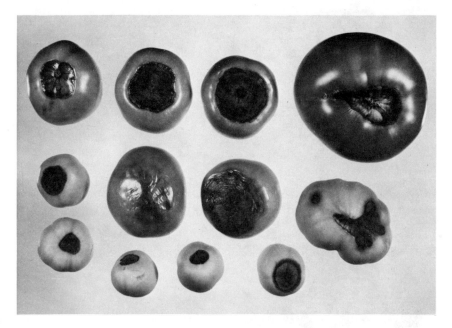

Figure 47. *The blossom end rot disorder in greenhouse tomatoes. Affected fruit ripen earlier and are worthless.*

equivalent to 8 pounds per 100 gallons of water. The sprayed nutrient is absorbed directly by the fruit and the leaves.

Internal Browning, Graywall, Blotchy Ripening.[15] These disorders all result in poor fruit color in the tomato. The terms are often used interchangeably.

Internal browning occurs when the plant and fruit are infected with tobacco mosaic virus. Fruit affected by internal browning have broad, brown streaks in the shoulder of the fruit. These are best seen if a slice is made through the shoulder of the fruit. The surface of the shoulder is rough, corrugated in appearance, and often sunken. This disorder may be controlled by using varieties resistant to mosaic and by maintaining cultural and sanitation practices in and around the greenhouse that will prevent tobacco mosaic virus infection. The depressing effect of tobacco mosaic virus on yields may be partially overcome by increasing the frequency and amount

[15] The authors acknowledge the helpful suggestions of Dr. Harry Murakishi, Professor of Botany and Plant Pathology, Michigan State University, East Lansing, Michigan 48824.

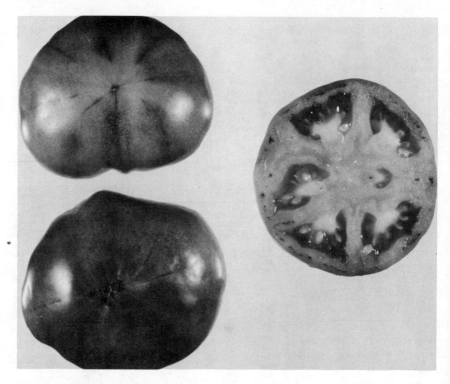

Figure 48. *The graywall and blotchy ripening disorder in greenhouse tomatoes. There are grayish-brown streaks in the outer wall and these areas fail to color resulting in blotchy fruit.*

of water and fertilizer applied. This increase should begin as soon as the first symptoms appear.

More recently, the inoculation of a mild strain of tobacco mosaic virus to tomato seedlings as a means of protection from the more virulent strains has been used in several European countries. This mild strain hardly produces any symptoms on the treated seedlings. Since there is a delaying effect of this mild strain of approximately three days, sowings should be made three to five days earlier to compensate for it. Significant increases in productivity have been achieved by this new technology (Table 30).

Green to mature-green fruit that have gray to grayish-brown streaks in the outer wall are affected with graywall (Fig. 48). The streaks may appear on any portion of the fruit wall, but are characteristically on the sides or base. The shoulders are generally smooth and not sunken as with internal browning.

Blotchy ripening refers to fruit that ripen or color unevenly (Fig. 48). When mature-green or green graywall fruit ripen, the areas which have brown streaks fail to color. Graywall is thus the color disorder that affects green or mature-green fruit; blotchy ripening refers to the same disorder in ripe or ripening fruit.

Several factors, independently or in combination, cause graywall and blotchy ripening. These include low light intensities, low temperatures, high soil moisture, high nitrogen levels, and low potassium levels. Varieties differ greatly in susceptibility. Early spring and especially fall and winter crops are prone to this disorder. Using fruit varieties that inherently tend to ripen uniformly, maintaining high or adequate soil potassium levels and temperatures of 60°F or above, and carbon dioxide enrichment all tend to alleviate the frequency and severity of these color disorders.

Diseases such as *Verticillium* and *Fusarium* wilt, bacterial diseases including canker and wilt, tobacco mosaic virus (tmv) and nematodes can be controlled by soil sterilization with live steam as described in an earlier section. It should be noted, however, that great progress is being made in developing varieties that now have multiple resistance to these pathogens.

⊛ *Insect and Disease Control by Chemical Means.* Chemical control of tomato diseases by spraying, dusting or aerosol, and more recently by fogging devices is minimized in this book. Most diseases and nematodes can be effectively controlled by a combination of variety resistance combined with steam sterilization of the soil, sanitation, and proper manipulation of temperature, relative humidity, and air circulation and exchange. Fungicides may occasionally be useful and sometimes necessary in preventing a disease problem and as a supplement to good cultural practices, as for example, when the desired climatic conditions cannot be maintained inside a greenhouse because of outside weather conditions. A specific instance and dramatic example of control achieved by a fungicide is the recently identified *Fusarium* crown rot in the Cleveland, Ohio area. Drenches of "Difolatan" have been remarkably successful following steam sterilization.

Stem infections of *Botrytis cineria* (gray mold) often occur. This disease may be effectively controlled by a drench of Captan-Dyrene-Ferbam (two pounds of each per hundred gallons of water) applied at the rate of one cupful per plant on and around the lower two to four inches of the stem. Dusts or sprays (one pound per hundred gallons of water) of Botran applied to the stems are also effective. Registration of all these materials is subject to cancellation. Clearance for their use must be obtained from regulatory agencies.

Insecticides should be employed as preventatives and applied early enough to avoid a build-up of high insect populations. The best results are obtained when the insecticides are applied at air temperatures ranging between 70 and 80°F. Fungicides, however, should not be sprayed on tomato plants when temperatures exceed 85°F, otherwise burning of the foliage may occur. Sprays give better control at lower temperatures than do aerosols or fumigants. Greenhouses should be thoroughly fumigated or steamed with appropriate chemicals preparatory to starting a crop. If this is done effectively, insects and diseases seldom become a serious problem. Insecticides are available for insect control, but check with local and state officials before use. Directions on the label should be followed. The recommendations and clearances for uses of insecticides and fungicides on greenhouse tomatoes are frequently changed. Even the use of those mentioned herein may be prohibited.

Biological Control. Two of the major greenhouse tomato pests, red spider mite and white fly, are being successfully controlled in Denmark and Great Britain. Parasite control of red spider mite is being widely used, while the control of white fly has been more difficult since it requires a careful timing in the introduction of the parasite to the white fly population. In North America only limited use of the parasite to control white fly has been reported.

For the control of the white fly, the parasitic wasp, *Encarsia formosa* is introduced into the greenhouse when the white flies begin to lay their eggs. In England, it is recommended that the parasitic nymphs be introduced as soon as the first flies are seen. The parasitic wasp deposits her eggs in the nymphs of the white fly. The eggs hatch and feed on the nymphs and emerge as adults.

The control agent for the red spider mite is the parasitic mite, *Phytoseiulus persimilis.* This mite originated from South America and feeds on the eggs, nymphs, and adults of the red spider mite.

The success in the biological control of greenhouse insects is dependent on the careful use of chemicals that will not harm the parasites that are in use. Insecticides have generally been found harmful to natural parasites, whereas fungicides have negligible effects. Morestan (quinomethionate) can be used in the greenhouse without damage to the white fly parasite, while the chemical Pirimor can be used without damage to the red spider mite parasite. Studies are in progress for the biological control of aphids. Biological control of the white fly and red spider mite is accredited with a 10 percent increase in yield of tomatoes (Table 30).

The cabbage looper, generally thought of as a field pest, has been found recently in greenhouses especially on fall grown tomato crops. The adult grayish moths fly at night and gain entry into greenhouses through open vents. The adults do no damage. However, the eggs hatch, and the larvae damage both leaves and fruit. The use of ultra-violet traps (Fig. 49) or home made traps such as a 200 watt bulb and a pan of water beneath attracts the moth and eliminates it prior to its laying eggs.

⊛ *Watering and Fertilizing Spring Crops.* Top yields of high-quality greenhouse tomatoes cannot be obtained if fruiting plants become deficient in moisture or mineral nutrients. Long sustained production is accomplished only by timely watering and generous feeding with soluble mixtures of nitrogen, phosphorus, and potash in proper proportions. One of the best methods of adding soluble

Figure 49. *An ultra-violet insect trap, particularly useful for control of the cabbage looper.*

Figure 50. *A properly nourished tomato plant. Note the closely spaced and large flower and fruit clusters, the thick stem, and large leaves.*

plant food is in the irrigation water. Since a precipitate results from mixing di-ammonium phosphate and mono-potassium phosphate in water, the mixture of these fertilizers in the irrigation water should be avoided. The precipitant may clog the nozzles or the fine holes of the drip hoses. Separate use of the two fertilizers in the irrigation water followed by proper flushing of the system is suggested. Fertilizer salts containing no chlorides, sodium, or sulfates are recommended. These include di-ammonium phosphate, mono-potassium phosphate, ammonium nitrate, potassium nitrate, and urea. Using these fertilizers prevents the dangers of salt accumulation in the soil (Tables 11, 12).

A satisfactory fertilizer and irrigation program should produce thick-stemmed tomato plants. Leaves should be dark green, flower clusters large, and fruit clusters closely spaced (Fig. 17, 18, 19, 20). A properly nourished plant's stem should be one-half inch thick at a point six to eight inches below the growing tip (Fig. 50).

Four or five large clusters of fruit exert a great demand for all available food reserves in the tomato plant. If nutrients or soil moisture are in short supply, the newly developing flowers will not set fruit, the diameter of the new stem growth becomes smaller, and the flower number is reduced. One or more clusters of fruit may be partially or completely lost before the competition for nutrients is relieved by removal of the ripening fruit from the bottom clusters. This results in greatly reduced yields and a short supply of fruit during critical periods of the harvest season.

Fertilizing schedules for early and late spring crops of greenhouse tomatoes are outlined in Tables 12 and 13. These schedules were formulated using Michigan-Ohio Hybrid; and, therefore, if other varieties are used, an alteration in the fertilizer schedule should be made. Varieties that are earlier and less vigorous than

TABLE 11. Changes in nutrient levels of greenhouse soils during growth of a late spring tomato crop with and without fertilizer added during the growth of the crop (Spring 1958).[a]

	No fertilizer added during growth of the crop					Fertilizer added during growth of the crop				
Date of sampling	pH	Soluble salts[b] ("K" value)	Pounds per acre N	P	K	pH	Soluble salts[b] ("K" value)	Pounds per acre N	P	K
March 21	7.3	77	44	136	410	7.3	78	44	146	425
April 21	7.6	60	39	145	605	6.9	70	44	225	720
May 22	7.5	19	11	190	117	6.6	60	44	450	450
June 21	7.8	20	2	123	176	6.7	70	88	420	1500
July 21	7.7	18	5	141	175	7.1	40	44	420	1300

[a] These studies conducted in cooperation with Dr. R. E. Lucas, Department of Crops and Soil Science, Michigan State University, East Lansing, Michigan 48824.
Soil nutrients determined by the Spurway "active" method.
[b] "K" value for soluble salts equals conductivity in mhos $\times$ 10^{-5}, for a 1 to 2 soil-water extraction.

TABLE 12. Fertilizer program for greenhouse tomatoes that received preplanting and supplemental fertilizer applications—early spring experimental crop, East Lansing, Michigan, 1959 (November 7, 1958, to July 15, 1959).

Date of Application	Pounds per acre			Pounds of fertilizer applied per acre during growth of the crop		
				Di-ammonium phosphate plus mono-potassium phosphate [c]	Potassium nitrate	Ammonium nitrate
	N	P$_2$O$_5$	K$_2$O			
Preplanting						
Manure [a]	1,000	500	1,000	—	—	—
0–20–20 [b]	—	300	300	—	—	—
During Growth						
March 27–April 9	92	208	244	400	400	—
April 10–April 23	69	156	183	300	300	—
April 24–May 7	118	78	157	150	300	200
May 8–May 21	103	—	132	—	300	200
May 22–June 4	103	—	132	—	300	200
June 5–June 12	103	—	132	—	300	200
Total for the crop	1,588	1,242	2,280	850	1,900	800

[a] The equivalent of 100 tons of manure added per acre. Nitrogen valued at 10, phosphate at 5 and potash at 10 pounds per ton.
[b] The equivalent of 1500 pounds of 0–20–20 fertilizer applied per acre.
[c] Equal parts by weight.

Michigan-Ohio Hybrid would require advancing the schedule 10 to 14 days as shown in Tables 12 and 13, while varieties that mature later should be delayed a week.

An irrigation program for an early spring crop is shown in Table 14. Such frequent irrigation may necessitate the furrow system where the water is confined to the plant row. Recently introduced drip systems would be admirably adapted to such high frequency irrigation programs. Irrigation pipes in traditional systems are often lowered from an overhead position (Fig. 37) to near the ground level (Fig. 51) to avoid excessive moisture on the foliage during the late fruiting period.

TABLE 13. Fertilizer program for greenhouse tomatoes that received preplanting and supplemental fertilizer applications—late spring experimental crop, East Lansing, Michigan, (December 23, 1957, to July 17, 1958).

				Pounds of fertilizer applied per acre during growth of the crop	
Date of Application	Pounds per acre			Di-ammonium phosphate plus mono-potassium phosphate [c]	Potassium nitrate
	N	P$_2$O$_5$	K$_2$O		
Preplanting					
Manure [a]	1,000	500	1,000	—	—
0–20–20 [b]	—	300	300	—	—
During Growth					
April 21–May 4	20	104	34	200	—
May 5–May 18	80	416	136	800	—
May 19–June 1	92	208	244	400	400
June 2–June 15	92	208	244	400	400
June 16–June 29	98	104	298	200	600
June 30–July 11	52	—	176	—	400
Total for the crop	1,434	1,840	2,432	2,000	1,800

[a] The equivalent of 100 tons of manure added per acre. Nitrogen valued at 10, phosphate at 5 and potash at 10 pounds per ton.
[b] The equivalent of 1500 pounds of 0–20–20 fertilizer applied per acre.
[c] Equal parts by weight.

These schedules have given high sustained production through eight fruit clusters for a late spring crop (Table 3) and through twelve clusters for an early spring crop (Table 14). High yields were maintained through twelve clusters with desirable fruit numbers and size. Yields of almost nineteen pounds per plant (eighty-eight tons per acre) have been obtained for a late spring crop. Close to twenty-five pounds per plant (over one hundred tons per acre) have been harvested for an early spring crop with the fertilizer schedules given in Tables 12 and 13.

Recommendations for fertilizing a spring crop of soil grown greenhouse tomatoes follow:

(1) From transplanting until plants have 10 to 15 fruit set, use 1:1 mixture of di-ammonium phosphate and mono-potassium phosphate. Just before or with the first irrigation, apply 150

pounds of the mixture per acre. Repeat the application when the plants are watered at 10-day to 2-week intervals.

(2) After 10 to 15 fruit have set and until 4 or 5 good clusters have set, use both the di-ammonium and the mono-potassium phosphate mixture and potassium nitrate. Seventy-five to 100 pounds per acre of each is applied at 7- to 10-day intervals.

(3) After 4 or 5 fruit clusters have set and until the plants are topped, discontinue the phosphate mixture and use potassium nitrate and ammonium nitrate or urea. Fifty to 100 pounds per acre of each may be applied at weekly intervals. The amount should depend on sunlight, results of soil test for nitrate nitrogen, plant vigor, and heaviness of fruiting. Where high potash fertilization is practiced, magnesium deficiencies resulting in light green or yellow spots on the older leaves may appear. If so, add magnesium sulfate at the rate of 300

TABLE 14. Irrigation program for an early spring crop of greenhouse tomatoes.[a]

Week	Number of applications	Gallons per plant	Inches per week
March 23–27	1	2	0.74
March 30–April 3	1	1	0.37
April 6–10	1	1	0.37
April 3–17	2	2	0.74
April 20–24	2	2	0.74
April 27–May 1	3	3	1.11
May 4–8	3	5	1.85
May 11–15	3	5	1.85
May 18–22	3	6	2.22
May 25–29	3	6	2.22
June 1–5	3	6	2.22
June 8–12	3	6	2.22
June 15–19	3	6	2.22
June 22–26	3	6	2.22
June 29–July 3	3	6	2.22
July 6–10	3	6	2.22
July 13–17	3	6	2.22

[a] Crop seeded November 7, 1958, transplanted to ground bed January 10 and harvest terminated July 15, 1959.

Figure 51. *Irrigation lines lowered to near the ground level. This avoids excessive moisture on the foliage and accompanying diseases during the fruiting period. Note that bottom leaves have been removed.*

to 500 pounds per acre. Dolomitic limestone may be used on slightly acid soils. Where the calcium content in the soil is low, soft fruit may result. This can be corrected by weekly applications of 100 pounds per acre each of calcium nitrate ($Ca[NO_3]_2$) and potassium nitrate (KNO_3) and 50 pounds per acre of ammonium nitrate (NH_4NO_3).

The above suggestions apply to greenhouse tomatoes grown under traditional soil conditions and irrigation facilities. Drip irrigation systems are ideal for high frequency irrigation and precise placement of water soluble fertilizer. They would greatly facilitate programming of fertilizer applications using the above recommended schedule.

If the above program is carefully followed for spring crops, high early and total yields can be expected (Tables 3 and 15). Sustained yields of one and a half to two pounds of fruit for each cluster can be produced (Fig. 19, 20). For an early spring crop having twelve to fourteen clusters per plant, this should give twenty to twenty-five pounds of fruit per plant. Late spring crops having eight to ten clusters per plant should produce fifteen to eighteen pounds per plant.

The above amounts of fertilizer are for maximum productivity. They are recommended because the cost of fertilizer is a small percentage of the total production cost. Growers of greenhouse tomatoes should not risk a nutrient deficiency. The amounts recommended will not cause an accumulation of salts, nor will they reduce yields.

The pounds of nutrients removed per acre are appreciable. Three hundred and fifty pounds of nitrogen, one hundred and five pounds of phosphorus, and five hundred and eighty pounds of potassium were found in the vines and fruit of a one hundred ton tomato crop in Michigan. Corresponding values for a forty-eight ton crop in Ohio showed a total removal of three hundred and seventy-nine pounds of nitrogen, one hundred and one pounds of phosphorus,

TABLE 15. Pounds of marketable fruit, numbers of fruit, and size of fruit of 12 clusters of the Michigan–Ohio Hybrid and Ohio WR–7 Globe tomatoes grown according to procedures outlined in this report (Early spring crop, 1959).

	Michigan-Ohio Hybrid			Ohio WR–7 Globe		
Cluster number	Lbs. of fruit per cluster	No. of fruit per cluster	Size of fruit in ounces	Lbs. of fruit per cluster	No. of fruit per cluster	Size of fruit in ounces
1	1.4	4.2	5.5	1.2	2.7	7.0
2	2.2	5.4	6.8	2.3	4.4	8.2
3	2.2	6.3	5.7	2.3	5.9	6.4
4	2.0	6.6	4.7	2.3	6.1	6.5
5	2.3	6.7	5.6	2.3	5.4	6.9
6	2.5	6.7	6.3	2.4	5.8	6.8
7	2.6	7.4	5.7	2.2	5.8	6.6
8	2.4	7.3	5.6	1.9	5.0	6.4
9	1.9	5.7	5.4	1.7	4.2	5.5
10	1.7	4.9	5.5	1.4	4.0	6.3
11	1.6	4.8	5.4	1.4	3.6	5.4
12	1.8	4.7	6.1	1.5	3.9	6.5
Totals or means	24.6	5.9	5.7	22.9	4.7	6.5

and six hundred and sixteen pounds of potassium per acre. Losses from nitrification, denitrification, soil fixation, and leaching must also be considered.

⊛   *Soil Tests and Desirable Ranges for Soil Nutrients.* Fertilizer applications for greenhouse tomatoes should be based on soil and tissue tests. The values in Table 16 are suitable for most soils. These soil nutrient levels have been consistently associated with high productivity.

There is a wide range for most nutrient levels in soils over which

TABLE 16. Suggested soil nutrient levels for high yielding crops of greenhouse-grown tomatoes.

Nutrient or measurement	Method of extraction or procedure	Pounds per acre or measurement
pH	1–1 soil water	6.5–7.2
Nitrogen (NO$_3$–N)—lb./acre	0.018 N acetic acid	25–80
Phosphorus (P)—lb./acre	0.018 N acetic acid	80–300
Potassium (K)—lb./acre	0.018 N acetic acid	300–1000
Calcium (Ca)—lb./acre	0.018 N acetic acid	above 800
Magnesium (Mg)—lb./acre	0.018 N acetic acid	above 32
Phosphorus (Bray P$_1$) lb./acre [a]	0.025N HCl plus 0.03 N NH$_4$F	250–800
Potassium (exchangeable) lb./acre	1 N ammonium acetate	400–1200
Calcium (exchangeable) lb./acre	1 N ammonium acetate	above 1500
Magnesium (exchangeable) lb./acre	1 N ammonium acetate	above 200
Potassium (saturation)—percent	1 N ammonium acetate	5–8
Calcium (saturation)—percent	1 N ammonium acetate	above 50
Magnesium (saturation)—percent	1 N ammonium acetate	above 10
Total exchange capacity (m.e./100 g)	1 N ammonium acetate	10–50 [b]
Soluble salts ("K" value)	1–2 soil water	50–75

[a] The phosphorus (Bray P$_1$) test is not suitable for soils containing free calcium carbonate (lime) of high pH (7.5–8.2).
[b] The total exchange capacity may be much higher than given in this range. Values exceeding 100 m.e./100 g. may occur in heavy clay soils and those high in organic matter.

high yields can be expected. The most desirable level for each nutrient or variable listed (Table 17) depends on the season of the
year, amount of sunlight, organic matter content of the soil, soil
texture, stage of plant development and extent of fruiting, preva-
lence and severity of tobacco mosaic, levels of carbon dioxide in the
greenhouse atmosphere, the crop variety, and finally the appearance
of the plants. The latter should always be considered in the final
determination of fertilizer requirements.

The total exchange capacity of the soil greatly affects the frequency and rate of fertilization. Soils of high exchange capacity
"absorb" and require much more fertilizer than those of low exchange capacity.

A somewhat abbreviated and simplified set of desirable soil test
values has recently been proposed and is now widely accepted for
greenhouse tomatoes. These values, enumerated in Table 17, are
based on parts per million of air dried soil.

⊛   *The Saturated Soil Extract Method.* [16] More recently the Saturated Soil Extract (SSE) paste method has been used to evaluate
plant nutrient levels for greenhouse soils. This test method better

[16] The authors acknowledge the suggestions of Dr. Darryl Warncke, Assistant Professor
of Soil Science, Michigan State University.

TABLE 17. Michigan soil test analyses for greenhouse soils (based on
ppm of air dried soil).[a]

Available nutrient or measurement	Desired values
pH	6.5–7.2
Nitrogen (NO_3)	12–40
Phosphorus	40–150
Potassium	200–600
Calcium	above 600
Magnesium	above 100
Soluble salts	50–90
(K value for 1:2 ratio)	

[a] The desired values when expressed as ppm are one-half of the values expressed as
pounds per acre (see Table 16). (The authors acknowledge the assistance of Dr.
R. E. Lucas of the Crops and Soil Science Department, Michigan State University in the
preparation of this table.)

expresses the available nutrient status and has been found suitable for evaluating the levels of major nutrients and also those for sodium, chloride, and micronutrients. The nutrient content is expressed as concentration in the extract solution, rather than on a soil basis.

With the SSE method, freshly sampled greenhouse soil mixes are wetted to complete saturation with distilled water while gently mixing. Prior to the development of the SSE test, greenhouse soil samples were air dried, ground, and sieved. With the SSE procedure, greenhouse samples are handled as they are. The saturated soil samples are then allowed to equilibrate for two hours, and then the soil mix solution is extracted with a vacuum filter. The moisture content of the saturated soil mix is about four times that held at the permanent wilting point, and about two times that held at field capacity. Hence, the soluble salt concentration in the saturation extract is about one-fourth and one-half that in the soil mix solution at permanent wilting and at field capacity, respectively. Measurement of the salt and nutrient concentration in a saturated soil extract gives a value which takes into account the water-holding characteristics of the growing media and which can be related to plant response. The pH is determined on the saturated soil mix. All other analyses are performed on the saturation extract. With the SSE method, results can be made available within 24 hours and routinely within 48 hours, compared to former procedures which required 5 days. This new soil extract method provides a good measure of the nutrient content of the soil mix solution. It is equally well adapted for traditional greenhouse soils and modern artificial mixes. It is closely related to the nutrient concentrations the plant roots experience. The SSE method enables a determination of nutrient balance. Optimum nutrient levels for greenhouse tomatoes are given in Table 18.

Based on the SSE method, the amount of nitrogen, phosphorus, and potassium necessary to rise to the desired values is shown in Table 19, using the popular fertilizers.

⊛ *Desirable Nutrient Levels in Fresh Petiole Tissue.* A range of mineral nutrient composition values in fresh leaf petioles removed from productive tomato plants is listed in Table 20. The results are expressed as parts per million of extractable nutrients on a fresh or wet weight basis. The moisture content of the tissue ranged from

TABLE 18. Optimum nutrient levels for greenhouse tomatoes, expressed in ppm according to the Saturated Soil Extract (SSE) procedure.

Available nutrient or measurement	Desired values (ppm)
pH	5.8–6.8
Nitrogen (NO_3)	125–200
Phosphorus	8– 13
Potassium	175–275
Calcium	>250
Magnesium	> 60
Soluble Salts (mmhos)	1.50–3.00

ninety-three to ninety-five percent. Petiole samples were from the most recent fully expanded leaf.

These values again suggest that a wide range in nutrient composition within the plant is associated with high productivity. The stage of plant development and the magnitude of fruiting are the most significant factors determining optimum nutrient levels in fresh leaf petiole tissues. While nitrate-nitrogen, phosphorus, and calcium levels can be maintained by adequate fertilization during the growth of the crop, the trend is for potassium to increase and magnesium to decrease at the same time.

⊛ *Desirable Nutrient Levels for Dried Petiole Tissue.* Petiole samples are taken from the leaf immediately below the last developing flower cluster which is usually the most recent, fully developed leaf. After drying in a 160°F oven, the mineral nutrient content is determined. Total nitrogen, potassium, and spectrographic analyses of the other essential mineral nutrients found in dried leaf petioles constitute perhaps the most reliable approach to solving nutrient problems and evaluating the nutritional status of a growing crop. The ranges listed in Table 21 were those associated with satisfactory plant growth and fruiting. The values for potassium and molybdenum are somewhat higher than those reported elsewhere for tomatoes and other crops, but leaf samples were not comparable.

Additional analyses have been conducted on leaf petioles of greenhouse-grown tomatoes from several locations (Table 22). The same sampling technique, petioles from the first leaf subtending the

latest developing flower cluster, was employed in all instances. These
values suggest that a very wide range of mineral nutrient levels may
be associated with high production in greenhouse tomatoes. Nutrient
levels in leaf petioles are a function of location and soil type, season
of the year, stage of plant development, and variety. The levels re-

TABLE 19. Rates of fertilizer required to increase the various plant
nutrients to the listed values based on the Saturated Soil
Extract (SSE) test.

Formula	Name	lbs/A
Nitrogen—to raise 10 ppm		
7–40–6	MagAmp	315
10–0–0		220
13–0–44	Potassium Nitrate	170
17–0–0	Calcium Nitrate	130
20–0–0		110
21–0–0	Ammonium Sulfate	100
21–53–0	Diammonium Phosphate	100
33–0–0	Ammonium Nitrate	65
45–0–0	Urea	45
Phosphorus—to raise 2 ppm		
0–20–0	Superphosphate	870
7–40–6	MagAmp	435
0–46–0	Treble Superphosphate	378
0–52–24	Monopotassium phosphate	335
21–53–0	Diammonium phosphate	328
Potassium—to raise 20 ppm		
7–40–6	MagAmp	378
0–0–20		126
0–0–30		74
13–0–44	Potassium Nitrate	59
0–0–50	Potassium Sulfate	50
0–0–60	Potassium Chloride	47
pH—to raise soil pH one unit (e.g. 5.3 to 6.3) Limestone required per acre in lbs.		
	Sandy loam	1740
	Loam	3480
	Clay loam or peat	5220

TABLE 20. Range in values of acetic acid extractable nutrients in fresh leaf petioles subtending the latest open flower cluster in productive crops of greenhouse-grown tomatoes.

Nutrients	Parts per million (ppm) in leaf petiole
Nitrate-nitrogen (NO_3–N)—ppm	600–1,500
Phosphorus (P)—ppm	200–400
Potassium (K)—ppm	3,000–8,000
Calcium (Ca)—ppm	750–1,500
Magnesium (Mg)—ppm	300–1,200

TABLE 21. Range in values of mineral nutrient levels in dried leaf petioles subtending the latest open flower cluster in productive crops of greenhouse-grown tomatoes.

Nutrient	Composition of leaf petioles (dry weight basis)	
	Percent	Parts per million
Nitrogen (N)	2.50 – 3.50	25,000– 35,000
Phosphorus (P)	0.50 – 1.00	5,000– 10,000
Potassium (K)	6.00 –10.00	60,000–100,000
Calcium (Ca)	1.25 – 3.00	12,500– 30,000
Magnesium (Mg)	0.30 – 1.00	3,000– 10,000
Sodium (Na)	0.02 – 0.40	200– 4,000
Manganese (Mn)	0.005 – 0.02	50– 100
Iron (Fe)	0.002 – 0.01	20– 100
Copper (Cu)	0.0005– 0.0025	5– 25
Boron (B)	0.002 – 0.004	20– 40
Zinc (Zn)	0.002 – 0.02	20– 200
Molybdenum (Mo)	0.0001– 0.0005	1– 5

ported for greenhouse-grown tomatoes in Cleveland, Ohio, were associated with excellent growth and heavy fruiting at the time of sampling.

The effects of carbon dioxide enrichment on reducing levels of potassium, calcium, and magnesium were apparent in the John Hoag and Sons planting in Elyria, Ohio. Severe yellow blotching of the leaves of fruiting plants occurred on the plants grown in an enriched atmosphere of carbon dioxide. The Jim Ellison greenhouse reported blossom-end rot of the fruit on WR–25, but not WR–3.

TABLE 22. Mineral nutrient levels of leaf petioles subtending the last developing inflorescence in greenhouse-grown tomatoes from various sources.

Location	Time of sampling	Variety	Grower	Percent in dry weight					Parts per million in dry weight						
				N	P	K	Ca	Mg	Na	Mn	Fe	Cu	B	Zn	Mo
San Antonio, Texas	January 1963	Manapal	Scientific Farms, Inc.	2.12	0.90	11.40	1.35	0.31	864	76	44	10	24	79	6
Tulsa, Oklahoma	April 1963	Step 390	Mingo Greenhouse Co.	3.34	0.96	8.40	3.44	1.27	691	46	37	9	32	26	11
Las Vegas, Nevada	February 1963	Indian River	Garden Farms, Inc.	2.89	0.80	9.96	1.98	0.52	410	85	50	16	30	87	8
Leamington, Ont. (Canada)	March 1963	M-O Hybrid	EM Farms, Ltd.	3.10	0.92	9.40	1.92	0.38	170	422	41	13	27	51	7
Cleveland, Ohio	March 1963	WR-7	Thomas Wolfe	3.02	0.90	9.56	2.77	0.55	460	508	16	18	43	84	9
Cleveland, Ohio	March 1963	WR-7	Walter McAlister	3.06	0.93	8.40	2.39	0.48	283	188	31	16	31	60	9
Elyria, Ohio	April 1964	WR-7 + CO_2	John Hoag and Son	2.36	0.95	5.80	1.54	0.21	864	247	44	16	30	103	6
Elyria, Ohio	April 1964	WR-7 − CO_2	John Hoag and Son	2.34	0.75	6.90	2.02	0.35	1152	140	50	13	26	60	7
Lubbock, Texas	September 1964	WR-3	Jim Ellison	2.58	1.09	4.34	1.72	0.64	1920	94	88	19	38	95	7
Lubbock, Texas	September 1964	WR-25	Jim Ellison	2.58	0.92	4.24	1.44	0.70	2192	80	91	17	38	75	6
Alice, Texas	January 1967	Manapal	James A. Gibson	1.70	0.63	8.96	3.37	0.60	831	162	49	15	23	78	9
Robstown, Texas	May 1967	Manapal	Gordon Merritt	4.70	0.87	3.84	3.19	0.77	831	896	222	36	83	121	7
Grapevine, Texas	November 1968	Wolverine 119	Pan American Hydroponics	2.88	0.73	9.40	1.36	0.24	3332	148	71	16	32	8	8

The level of leaf calcium for WR–25 was significantly lower than that for WR–3.

As a general rule, the tomato plant's nitrogen requirement increases with increasing sunlight and longer days. The relative need for potassium increases with decreasing sunlight and shorter days. Thus, nitrogen is often in short supply for spring crops, while potassium may be the critical nutrient in the fall.

The final index of fertilizer need, however, is the plant. The thickness of the stem near the growing tip, the vigor and number of the newly developing flowers, the degree of fruit setting, and the leaf size and color should be watched closely. These features, in combination with the results of periodic soil and leaf tissue tests, the season of the year, and the amount of prevailing sunlight serve as the final guides for determining the proper amounts of fertilizer and water.

⊛   *Watering and Fertilizing Fall Crops.* The climatic pattern during the growth of fall tomato crops in Michigan and other temperate zone areas is opposite to that for spring crops. Growers in the northern states should water and fertilize the young plants frequently during August and early September when temperatures are high and sunlight is adequate. From October 15 to 20, plants should be topped and fruit setting terminated. Fruit which is set after October 20 will probably not mature by the time the crop is removed in December. Watering and fertilizing should be greatly reduced during October and usually discontinued completely by mid-November. Timely termination of vegetative growth and watering is essential in the growth of fall crops, for it enables the tomato plant to use the limited carbohydrates that are produced under conditions of insufficient sunlight for fruit production. There is usually a negative balance of light after November 1.

An excellent fertilizer for a fall crop is potassium nitrate, which may be added liberally (one hundred to two hundred pounds per acre per week) during late August and through September. If soil tests show a need for phosphorus, equal amounts of di-ammonium phosphate and mono-potassium phosphate may also be used. High potash levels during the fall and early winter will improve fruit quality. The tomato plant will also utilize the available sunlight more efficiently. As with spring crops, the needs for fertilizer and water usually occur together. Fall crops seldom benefit from fertilizer applied after October 15.

⊛ *Mulch for Top Yields of High-Quality Fruit.* Manure, as the exclusive source of organic matter for greenhouse tomato soils, is often expensive. It may also greatly increase the accumulation of soluble salts. The proper use of mulches will alleviate the problem of soluble salt accumulation, supply the necessary organic matter, and give greater control over soil nutrient levels during crop growth (Fig. 52).

Many other benefits result from mulching greenhouse tomatoes grown in conventional soil cultures. As more uniform soil moisture is maintained, there is less fruit cracking. Root extension is favored, since roots penetrate the surface soil under the mulch and even the lower layers of the mulch. Soil aeration is improved, and there is less soil compaction. Fruit on the lower clusters are protected from the spattering of soil particles during irrigation. The heavy first fruit clusters are also supported by the mulch and protected from direct contact with the soil. Moreover, mulches release large quantities of carbon dioxide to the greenhouse atmosphere. The concentration may be particularly increased during the early morning hours. Decomposing peanut hulls are an especially rich source of carbon dioxide.

For traditional soil culture, it is recommended that growers mulch with two to four inches of straw, hay, peanut hulls, rice hulls, or other suitable material. Fifteen to twenty tons per acre may be required, and they should be the type that is easily worked into the soil and broken down by soil organisms. Mulches should be free from weed seeds and toxic chemicals, such as those used in weed control. Peanut hulls are not recommended if the cropping system includes the growing of leaf lettuce, unless peanut hulls free of toxic chemicals are obtainable. In areas where rice hulls are available, treated rice hulls can be used for mulches. The only disadvantage is the slow decomposition as compared to other types.

An excellent mulching material used in the Cleveland, Ohio area is sugarcane litter, which is available as a baled and sterilized product. [17] Six to seven tons per acre are required at a cost of from two hundred and fifty to three hundred dollars. Sugarcane litter is used as a replacement for peanut hulls, which have recently been identified as carriers of *Rhizopus* fruit rot and nematodes. These pathogens have been a serious problem since 1960 in greenhouses

[17] U.S. Sugar Corporation, Clewiston, Florida 33440.

Figure 52. *Straw mulch 2 to 4 inches deep is applied along the rows. This adds organic matter, CO $_2$, reduces soil compaction and soil temperature and the incidence of* botrytis *mold on the fruit.*

where peanut hulls have been used. As sugarcane litter can lead to a nitrogen shortage similar to that formerly experienced with corn-cob mulches, additional nitrogen will have to be supplied.

Some growers specialize in tomatoes as a single annual spring crop. The ground beds are steam sterilized in late August, then planted in rye or ryegrass. This green manure crop is worked into the soil shortly before the new tomato crop is to be transplanted. In addition to increasing the soil organic matter, this procedure temporarily reduces the excess nitrogen released by sterilization, and binds it in organic form.

⊛ *Applying Fertilizer Solutions.* The most desirable and convenient approach is to feed concentrated fertilizer solutions into the irrigation system through an injector or proportioner. Tomato plants generally require both fertilizer and water at the same time; by this method, they can be added together. A given unit of fertilizer concentrate solution is metered into the line water stream for each unit or amount of water. This method provides a continuing supply of each nutrient, which can be changed progressively as the crop develops or as outside weather conditions change.

The nutrient salts most commonly utilized to supply the various nutrients and the amounts of each per thousand gallons of water are listed in Table 23. Judicious manipulation of the amounts and combination of these salts metered into an irrigation system will provide soil nutrient levels sufficient to maintain optimal growth and fruiting. In many soils and artificial mixes adequately supplied with calcium and magnesium, potassium nitrate supplemented with ammonium nitrate and di-ammonium and mono-potassium phosphates (Tables 12, 13) is sufficient.

In western Europe, phosphate is added to the soil before planting. A liquid fertilizer feed mixture is then prepared containing one hundred pounds of potassium nitrate, twenty pounds of urea, and forty-two pounds of Epsom salts (magnesium sulfate) in one hundred gallons of water. It is diluted at the rate of one gallon of the concentrate to one hundred and forty gallons of water when applied to the crop. Micronutrients, if needed, can be added according to the dilutions in Table 23.

TABLE 23. Fertilizer salts for greenhouse tomatoes—composition and dilutions for liquid feeding.

Carriers	Major Nutrients			Amount per 1000 gallons (lbs.)
	N	Percent P_2O_5	K_2O	
Ammonium nitrate	33			5–10
Potassium nitrate	14		44	10–20
Calcium nitrate	15			10–20
Mono-potassium phosphate		50	34	10–20
Mono-ammonium phosphate	11	48		10–20
Di-ammonium phosphate	21	54		10–20
Magnesium sulfate				10–20

Micronutrients	Amount per 1000 gallons (grams)
Iron chelate (iron)	100
Sodium borate (boron)	8
Manganese sulfate (manganese)	8
Zinc sulfate (zinc)	1
Copper sulfate (copper)	1/2
Molybdic acid (molybdenum)	1/10

❧ HARVESTING, HANDLING, MARKETING

◎ *Fruit Quality.* The most outstanding feature of the greenhouse tomato is its consistently high quality. Color, shape, size, absence of defects, general appearance, firmness, and grade are reproducible as precise control and regulation of temperatures both before and after harvest are possible. Optimal color development occurs at 60 to 72°F. Tomatoes produced by the nutrient film culture technique (to be described later) have been noted to ripen more uniformly, are slightly firmer, and less "boxy" than those grown in peat culture.

High quality is related to the time of harvest. Greenhouse tomatoes should be harvested only after they have begun to ripen (color) on the vine. The fruit is usually harvested three times a week, but may be picked daily during peaks and in hot weather. Frequent harvest enables the grower to pick at optimal ripeness and reduce the incidence of cracking.

Greenhouse tomatoes in America are generally harvested too green, presumably to insure a firmer ripe fruit. The potential premium in quality, however, is seldom achieved by such a practice. European and Japanese growers leave the fruit on the vine until almost full color. Consumer preference studies indicate that fruit showing one hundred percent, or near one hundred percent, color are clearly preferred over those showing forty percent, twenty percent, or no color (Frontispiece).

Harvest requires hand labor (Fig. 53) and personal selection of each fruit. There is no immediate prospect of mechanizing harvest.

◎ *Fruit Transport Systems.* The most common method of transport of harvested tomatoes is to either hand carry, or move the filled containers on small carts from the picking rows to a central roadway. Some labor saving innovative transport systems from the rows have been designed. In Europe, there has been an immense development in the transport system to move products in and out of the greenhouse growing area. For the tomato, the rail system was found to be most economical and efficient (Fig. 54). The capital and annual maintenance costs were low, and the system can be used for the

Figure 53. *Greenhouse tomato harvest requires hand labor and personal selection of each fruit. These picking carts hold 12 eight-pound baskets of fruit and greatly reduce walking time for the harvest crew.*

harvest as well as for the cultural operation of the crop. Efficiency of the operation is improved by moving things quickly, thus saving time; making it easy to move the product, and therefore less tiring for the operator; and reducing the damage to the product being transported.

In the two types of rail systems described below, the transportation takes place on a permanent installation. The installation normally consists of heating pipes or specially made rails over which the trolley can run (Fig. 55). In the over-the-crop system, the heating pipes are suspended between the rows to which the trolleys run and is commonly referred as suspended trolley. In the rail system alongside or between the crop, the trolley is moved manually or motor driven over heating pipes near the ground (Fig. 54). The platforms are adjustable in height, and can be used for harvesting, pruning, and lowering of the vines (Fig. 55). Tomatoes can, thus, be harvested from a sitting position. There is no need for moving the picking baskets or the trolley where the trolley is motorized. In the suspended rail system, the platform is also adjustable so the height of the baskets can be at the convenience of the operator.

Figure 54. *The rail system using heating pipes makes an economical and efficient transport system within a greenhouse.* (STATE FARM MOSCOW, U.S.S.R.).

In both rail systems, the fruit baskets are transferred to a motorized car and hauled to the packing area. In the suspended system, the rails often continue to the packing area.

More recently, a large number of growers in Holland have installed variations of belt conveyor systems in the glasshouse. Baskets of fruit are gently emptied on the conveyor, and are moved to the grading and packing area.

Experiments on the use of flotation systems are also underway. With this system, a water trough is constructed along the main pathway of the houses where the fruits are being harvested. The pickers empty their baskets into the troughs. The flowing water carries the fruit to a roller elevator where the fruit passes over a drier prior to reaching the grading and packing area.

⊛ *Single Cluster Culture.* Consideration has been given to single cluster tomato production in western Europe. The plants, spaced eight inches apart, are topped two leaves above the first fruit cluster. Since there is little difference in ripening time between the first and last fruit of a cluster, mechanical harvesting may be possible. Studies in England with single one cluster plants spaced 9 x 9 inches

Figure 55. *A permanent trolley system with height adjustable platforms for pruning, training and lowering the vines.*

indicated that it was not economically feasible to grow tomatoes by this method. Extreme caution was necessary in the use of the proper cultivar, and in keeping the foliage dry to reduce disease.

Limited studies on production techniques with no comparative costs of production were made at the Michigan Agricultural Experiment Station (Fig. 56). The cultivar Jet Star was found best suited to this type of culture when grown to two-clusters, with plant spacings of 12 x 12 inches, supported by a wire frame 10 inches above the ground, watered by a drip hose, and grown in highly fertile soil. High fertility (25% greater than used for regular growing of greenhouse tomatoes), as well as greater frequency of watering, were necessary. One and a half pounds of marketable fruit per plant were harvested from the Jet Star cultivar. Comparable yields of marketable fruit per plant from four varieties are given in Table 24. Green fruit were not included.

Figure 56. *Single cluster culture of greenhouse tomatoes. Plants spaced 12 x 12 inches and supported by a wire frame 12 inches off the ground.*

The use of the plant regulator, ethephon, enhances greenhouse tomato yields by increasing the production of ripe fruit for the first and total harvests. This chemical, developed by Amchem Products, Inc.,[18] when applied to tomato plants two weeks prior to harvest, triggers the release of ethylene from the plant and also adds to the

[18] Ambler, Pennsylvania

TABLE 24. Average yield of marketable fruits per plant from four cultivars grown to two clusters and at a spacing of 12 x 12 inches.

| Cultivar | Transplanting dates | | | Average of 3 dates | Fruit size |
| | Feb. 24 | May 20 | Aug. 6 | | |
	oz	oz	oz		oz
Jet Star	21.3	26.4	25.2	24.3 [a]	5.2
Bonus	10.3	26.1	19.9	18.8 [ab]	5.3
Terrific	11.0	25.2	22.4	19.6 [ab]	5.1
Strain 173	14.8	19.9	17.1	17.3 [b]	4.6

Average in column with different letters differ significantly at 5% level.

release of ethylene. The released ethylene accelerates fruit ripening and coloration. Growers are, thus, able to produce a larger amount of marketable ripe fruit within two weeks.

Details of a study at Michigan Agricultural Experiment Station are given in Table 25. When 5 percent of the fruits were in the "breaker stage," ethephon was sprayed at a rate of 1000 ppm. Fruit were harvested two weeks later when the unsprayed plots were 40 percent ripe. The second harvest followed a week later. The use of preharvest spray of 1000 ppm of ethephon gave a higher percentage of ripe fruit the first harvest for both May 20 and August 6 plantings. While fruit size was smaller for the sprayed plants, the quality did not appear to be impaired.

High density plant populations offer possibilities for multiple and continuous cropping. The system may lend itself to the use of machines or machine aids in harvesting. Additional concentrations of ripe fruit harvest may be achieved with sprays of ethephon. The more apparent benefits would be a reduction of labor and costs relating to pollination, tying, pruning, and hand transplanting.

Ethephon sprays may also be applied to upper parts of traditionally grown greenhouse tomato plants near the end of the harvest period. The treatment encourages earlier and more uniform ripening, and there is improvement in overall quality compared to those not treated.

◉ *Post-Harvest Handling and Marketing.* Following harvest, tomatoes if not in full color may be held for a few days at 60 to 65°F for ripening and for short intervals at 50 to 55°F if fully ripe. Tomatoes should not be held in cold storage. It is important that the fruit be moved rapidly through marketing channels.

Most greenhouse tomatoes are packed as double layers in eight-pound cartons or baskets (Fig. 57), although single-layer packs are common in some areas. The product should be distinctly labeled on the package and by decals, or some trademark or other identification such as the inclusion of the green calyx on the harvested fruit. Fruits are picked with stem, and the stem trimmed with special snips or pruning shears flush with the top of the fruit. A small portion of the stem and calyx is thus attached to the fruit, but not sufficiently long to damage or puncture other fruit.

Growers should market only high-quality, vine-ripened tomatoes. Many small growers, especially those using hydroponic culture, sell independently and directly to a few stores or a single chain. Often

Figure 57. *The eight-pound greenhouse tomato carton. Note the descriptive cover.*

an attractive price is established and held for the entire season or crop. The majority of greenhouse tomatoes, however, are sold through cooperative marketing organizations (Fig. 58). Here the competition is severe from imported, shipped-in, repacked, and artificially ripened tomatoes, as well as from fruit which is vine ripened outdoors either locally or in distant areas.

Producers and the cooperatives with which they are associated in the major greenhouse tomato areas should take a new look at fruit maturity at harvest. Greenhouse tomatoes in the United States continue to be picked and marketed too green. The end product is not attractive either in appearance, texture, or eating quality. This is destroying one of the most compelling preferences for greenhouse-grown tomatoes over those grown in the open. Greenhouse tomatoes should be, in the true sense, vine ripened. Tomatoes picked too green miss the more important stage of ripening. During the vine ripening process, sugars, acids, and other flavor components move into the fruit to give the sweet and tangy taste, and the texture

TABLE 25. Effect of a preharvest spray of ethephon (1000 ppm) on concentration of fruit ripening, total yield per plant, and fruit size.

	Date of transplanting									
	May 20					August 6				
	Ripe fruits		Green fruits	Yield per plant	Fruit size	Ripe fruits		Green fruits	Yield per plant	Fruit size
Treatment	First harvest	Second harvest				First harvest	Second harvest			
	percent	percent	percent	oz	oz	percent	percent	percent	oz	oz
Not Sprayed	43.7	29.6	26.7	24.7	5.6	41.9	48.0	10.1	21.2	4.3
Sprayed	65.8	24.1	10.1	24.3	5.2	81.0	18.0	0.1	21.1	3.8

Figure 58. *A central packing plant for a small greenhouse tomato marketing cooperative.*

associated with properly vine-ripened fruit. Many newly established growers in areas of less concentrated production are realizing a premium for vine-ripened tomatoes. This practice needs to be re-established in the major producing areas.

ᚦ COSTS AND RETURNS: THE ECONOMICS OF PRODUCTION

Many growers have been tempted in recent years by the prospects of quick profits and reportedly high returns from sales of greenhouse tomatoes. As one grower puts it, "You are not going to get rich in the tomato business and you are not going to make big money in a hurry." No agricultural enterprise is beset with more financial and production hazards. The initial investment is high; the industry is

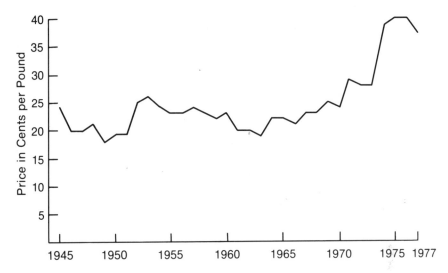

Figure 59. *Average yearly returns (1945–1977) to the grower in cents per pound for greenhouse tomatoes after deducting 3 to 5 cents per pound for the package, packaging, grading and marketing. These prices represent averages for all grades marketed through three large cooperatives in the United States and Canada and combine values for spring and fall crops.*

threatened by rising costs of production, escalating fuel prices and uncertainties, added environmental and regulatory constraints, shortages and rising costs for labor, and increasingly severe competition from the local and shipped-in commodity. Prices of the marketed product did not change appreciably from 1945 to 1970 (Fig. 59). Meanwhile, costs of production rose steadily. Success during this 25 year period can be attributed only to the remarkable developments in production technology which resulted in higher yields. Prices began an upward trend in 1971, and have continued through 1977 (Fig. 59). This has not been sufficient, however, to compensate for a 3-fold increase in heating costs and a doubling of the cost of labor during the 1971 to 1977 period.

It is much easier to estimate gross returns than expenses in greenhouse tomato production. In the late 1960's, some growers on the Isle of Guernsey; in the Cleveland, Ohio area; in Leamington, Ontario; in Michigan; and in one or two instances in Texas; when fall and spring crops are added together, achieved approximately one hundred tons per acre per year. This is twenty-five thousand eight-pound baskets per acre. At a conservative price of two dollars per-basket (before deducting twenty-six cents for packaging, transportation, and marketing), this was a gross return of fifty thousand dollars per acre. Although gross returns exceeding fifty thousand dollars per acre per year were realized, average production was generally much lower.

Production costs and returns for greenhouse-grown tomatoes have changed dramatically in the 1970's, compared to the relative stability characteristic of the 1950's and 1960's. Expenses per acre per year for the late 1960's were estimated, as given in Table 26.

The interest on the investment depended on the nature of the greenhouse (plastic, fiberglass, glass) and accessories. Heating and fuel costs were based on current prices of gas and coal in Michigan and adjoining states and were, of course, much less farther south or in the Southwest. Labor costs varied, but the trend was toward progressive increases. Other items were largely fixed charges (Tables 27, 28).

The marked increases in costs that occurred from the late 1960's to the 1975–78 period may be noted by a comparison of the values given in Tables 26 and 29. These data apply to Michigan and Ohio and adjoining areas, but are characteristic of the greenhouse tomato industry, in general, both in the U.S. and abroad. Overall costs doubled with a three-fold increase in the price of fuel for heating. Increases in prices of tomatoes (Fig. 59) have generally lagged behind the increases in cost of gas and oil. Furthermore, prices for marketed fruit received by growers have not kept pace with total production costs.

TABLE 26. Estimate costs per acre per year for growing greenhouse tomatoes in conventional soil culture, late 1960's.

Investment	Costs/acre/year
Interest on the investment	$ 6,000–$10,000
Heating and fuel (includes steam sterilization)	8,000– 10,000
Labor	10,000– 13,500
Containers and labels	2,500– 2,500
Electricity	300– 300
Fertilizer and twine	300– 500
Miscellaneous	500– 1,000
Totals	$27,600–$37,800

TABLE 27. Greenhouse tomato production costs during the 1960's under glass (per acre, per year).[a]

Buildings		Single crop cost	
Interest	$5,400	Seed (2 ozs.)	$ 80.00
		Germ. Seed	60.00
Taxes	500	Plant Bands	70.00
		Fertilizer	400.00
Insurance	750	Manure	325.00
		Twine	100.00
	6,650	Sprays	100.00
		Labor	5,500.00 (2 men full time)
Maintenance	600	Heat	3,500.00
		Electricity	400.00
	7,250	Sterilization	600.00
		Mulch	75.00
Depreciation	5,000	Water	250.00
		Commun.	100.00
		Misc.	1,000.00
			$12,160.00
		Crop	12,160.00
		⅔ Building	5,250.00
		⅔ Depreciation	3,332.00
			$20,742.00

[a] These figures were arrived at in a discussion with a large number of established tomato growers at the Short Course on Commercial Greenhouse Vegetable Production, held October 15–19, 1962, at Michigan State University. Prepared by Norman J. Smith (Bridgeton, N.J. 08302) and R. Sheldrake, Jr. (Cornell University, Ithaca, N.Y. 14850). They were further reviewed in detail and "agreed upon" at the Short Course on Commercial Greenhouse Production, October 15, 1964. Interest rates and labor costs for 1969 were estimated at from twenty-five to fifty percent above the 1964 figures indicated.

The most viable means for increasing profit margins for producers of greenhouse tomatoes is to increase yields. It centers upon increasing yields per unit area, per unit time, and/or multiple cropping schedules that optimize gross revenue per year per unit of producing area. Studies at Purdue University[19] have revealed that 2.5 pounds of tomatoes per square foot were required to amortize operational costs for a single cropping schedule. It would be lower under alternative multiple cropping systems.

[19] Sullivan, G. H. and J. L. Robertson. 1974. Purdue Agricultural Experiment Station Research Bulletin 908.

TABLE 28. Greenhouse tomato production costs during the 1960's under plastic (per acre, per year).[a]

Buildings		Single crop cost	
Interest	$1,500.00	Seed	$ 80.00
		Germ. Seed	60.00
Taxes	150.00	Bands	70.00
		Fertilizer	600.00
Insurance	150.00	Manure	350.00
		Twine	120.00
Maintenance	1,250.00	Sprays	100.00
		Labor	5,500.00
Depreciation	2,000.00	Heat	2,800.00
		Electricity	500.00
	$5,050.00	Sterilization	600.00
		Mulch	75.00
		Water	250.00
		Commun.	100.00
		Misc.	1,000.00
			$12,305.00
		Crop Cost	$12,305.00
		⅔ Fixed Cost	3,366.00
			$15,671.00

[a] It was decided at the Short Course (October 15, 1964) that the cost of marketing was from thirty-five to forty cents per eight-pound basket. This cost includes container, tissue paper, dividers, covers, and other supplies used in packaging, transportation to market, and selling costs (commissions).

TABLE 29. Estimated costs per acre, per year for growing greenhouse tomatoes in conventional soil culture, 1975–1978.

Investment	Costs/acre/year
Interest on the capital investment	$10,000–$13,000
Heating and fuel (includes steam sterilization)	20,000– 35,000 [a]
Labor	15,000– 20,000
Containers, electricity, fertilizer, water, twine, seed, etc.	5,000– 7,000
Totals	$50,000–$75,000

[a] Cost varies greatly as to type of fuel (oil, coal, gas) used. The use of coal for greenhouse heating is generally prohibited in the U.S. and some European countries.

Progressive greenhouse tomato growers now accept the reality that a profitable production program should aim at 100 tons or more of marketable tomatoes per acre per year. This magnitude of production has been demonstrated experimentally for both single and multiple cropping systems. A production level now exceeding 100 tons for a single crop (March–November) on approximately 100 acres has been achieved in Britain (Table 30). Important technological inputs have been pre-inoculation with tobacco mosaic virus (1971/72); use of peat modules or mattresses (1973/74); biological controls for white fly and red spider mites (1975/76). The next technological breakthrough in Britain may be the use of the nutrient film technique for growing the plants. Use of modern technologies (improved varieties, the "lay-down method" for plant stems, 20 meter free span houses, controlled watering and feeding, CO_2 enrichment, climate control, and better growing media) have given 120–140 tons per acre in Denmark. This has been for a single crop harvested from late March to late November. Progressive growers in the Cleveland, Ohio area regularly produce 100–120 tons of tomatoes per acre per year using conventional soil culture and following a two crop per year system. Harvest of the spring crop begins by mid-March and continues until about July 15. The fall crop harvest begins in October and carries through December. New tobacco mosaic resistant varieties, alone, have accounted for a recent 10–20 percent increase in yields. Hydroponically grown tomatoes,

TABLE 30. Technology inputs and greenhouse tomato yields.[a]

Year	Tons/acre	Cents/lb	New Technologies Adopted
1968/69	73	19	————————
1969/70	71	18	————————
1970/71	72	20	————————
1971/72	83	21	TMV [b] pre-inoculation
1972/73	69	26	TMV inoculation failure
1973/74	85	30	Peat modules
1974/75	92	34	————————
1975/76	107	39	Parasites for white fly and spider mites
1976/77	107	41	————————

[a] Data adapted from those derived from Van Heyningen Bros. Ltd. Nurseries, Littlehampton, England.
[b] TMV=Tobacco Mosaic Virus.

following a two crop per year system under the almost ideal climatic conditions of San Diego County, California, have recently given a 175 ton/acre/year production record. Commercial yields approaching this record have also been obtained with sand culture near Tucson, Arizona, under high sunlight where the latest technologies for controlled environment agriculture developed at the Environmental Research Laboratories of the University of Arizona were utilized (Fig. 43).

ᢒᢇ LABOR SAVING DEVICES

Labor now represents almost 30 percent of the total cost of greenhouse tomato production (Table 29). It is down from almost 40 percent in the late 1960's. Nevertheless, the trend for the future will be an ever increasing investment unless labor saving devices are adopted. Innovations to reduce this cost outlay are being sought and quickly adopted. Automation in heating, in irrigation, in metering devices for applying fertilizers through the irrigation water, for ventilation, and in carbon dioxide enrichment has proceeded rapidly in recent years.

Conventional spraying equipment for insect and disease control is being rapidly replaced by fogging devices. A full range of fogging devices is now available.

Riding type rototillers for rapid and effective soil preparation are available (Fig. 60). These can be set at varying depths and for a small initial cost can take much of the drudgery out of this operation. Versatile types, such as the Cub Cadet, have been developed which can, with a proper framework, be adapted to greatly speed up other operations, such as transporting transplants and harvested fruits.

A four-wheel "bicycle cart" with two 2″ x 8″ x 10′ planks mounted two to four feet off the ground has been designed as a pruning and tying aid (Fig. 31). Standing on one end, the worker pulls it along the rows by using the overhead wires, or it can be made to operate on electricity.

Picking carts (Fig. 53) holding twelve eight-pound baskets each are used in many areas. They greatly reduce walking and speed up harvest. Pallets and mechanical fork lifts are used in some areas.

Automated pollination devices and irrigation systems such as

Figure 60. *A real labor saving device. This self-propelled riding rototiller, which can be adjusted for depth, greatly facilitates soil preparation and may, with an appropriately attached frame be used for transplanting transplants and other items in a greenhouse.* (HOLWERDA BROS. GREENHOUSES, GRAND RAPIDS, MICH.).

perforated hoses, drip hoses, trickle systems, and overhanging sprinkling systems, described earlier, also decrease the labor requirement. Growers tend to develop different labor saving aids for irrigation and fertilizer applications. In the Leamington, Ontario area, centralized winch-pulled slides with attached sprinklers are used.

Planting and transplanting of crops is labor intensive. Automatic seeding and transplanting devices have been developed and have received some acceptance (Fig. 61).

৯ GLASS VERSUS PLASTIC, RIGID PVC, OR FIBERGLASS GREENHOUSES

Much of the recent expansion in the acreage of greenhouse tomatoes in this country and abroad, particularly in the Mediterranean countries (France, Italy, Spain, Turkey, and Greece), Great Britain, Israel, Hungary, Japan, and Korea, is related to advancements in

Figure 61. *A mechanical aid in the transplanting of greenhouse tomatoes.*

the use of plastics, fiberglass and more recently, polyvinyl chloride (PVC). The construction costs for plastic are much less than those for glass or fiberglass. The costs of the latter two are comparable.

Spectral energy transmission from the sun through polyethylene plastic, PVC, or fiberglass greenhouses is entirely adequate for tomato plant growth. The light within plastic, rigid PVC, or fiberglass greenhouses is diffused while the transmission is direct through glass. Fewer growth cracks in the fruit are likely to occur in plastic or fiberglass greenhouses than in glass structures.

In regions frequented by violent hailstorms, fiberglass and rigid PVC, or plastic greenhouses are essential. This includes some parts of the Middle West, the eastern slope of the Rocky Mountains, and the Southwest. Hail can be a hazard in any area in the U.S. where glass greenhouses are built.

The plastic greenhouse, and to some extent the fiberglass and rigid PVC greenhouse, are essentially closed air systems. Hence, adequate ventilation, air exchange, carbon dioxide enrichment, and heat distribution must be provided. Most of the hazards associated with tomato culture in plastic and fiberglass greenhouses arise from difficulties in controlling humidity and temperature and the accompanying layer of condensate on the inside surface of the film. Plastics have a higher surface tension which results in the formation of condensation droplets while on glass the condensation forms a film of water.

Droplets of water reflect some of the solar radiation back to the sky, especially under direct sunlight conditions. Although some of the light is reflected by the condensation on the film, the transmission is not lower than glass because of the greater amount of opaque material in the form of trusses and purlins in the roof of a glass greenhouse.

The formation of condensation can be greatly reduced by spraying the surfactant *"Sunclear"* [20] or by use of non-drip PVC film. The use of Sunclear results in an even higher light transmission. Under overcast conditions without Sunclear, the transmission was 67% of the outside light, while with Sunclear it was 75%. Under bright or direct sunlight, there was 61% transmission without Sunclear. This was increased to 67% following its application.

A serious reduction in light transmission after the first year has been observed with fiberglass and PVC film. Dust and other foreign particles collect on the exposed glass fibers and are very difficult to remove. Non-static PVC which does not attract dust has been developed. Fiberglass is also now available with an acrylic content and surface treatment which gives it a long life without loss of light transmission and a lifting of the surface fibers. Its final durability, however, remains as yet unknown. Rigid Japanese PVC has also

[20] Solar Sunstill, Inc., Setauket, New York 11733.

been greatly improved and offers another alternative.

Another example of a closed air system house is the air inflated plastic or "bubble" [21] (Fig. 62). The Cleveland Greenhouse Growers Association cooperated with the Goodyear Tire and Rubber Company for three years to get the bubble structure off the ground. The company had the engineering technology for erecting air inflated enclosures but the structure had to be adapted for greenhouse tomato production which included heating, ventilation, and air conditioning.

The bubble resembles the fabric-type air building which has been on the market since the late 50's which uses low inflation pressures. It is made of a network of steel cables that are anchored to the ground at various intervals. Double 12-mil plastic is sealed to the cables. Dead air is sandwiched between the two layers of vinyl and serves as insulation. These structures span large areas, and at a low cost (50¢/square foot in 1972) cover them without the need for internal support such as pillars or tie downs (Fig. 63). Thus, it is economical to cover large areas. The bubble is one means of reducing construction costs, fuel requirements (up to 30%) and increasing the efficiency of labor. The automatically controlled environment will also reduce the labor requirement.

Special air-inflated low cost plastic houses have been designed by the Environmental Research Laboratories at the University of

[21] Environmental Structures, Inc., 7600 Wall Street, Cleveland, Ohio 44125.

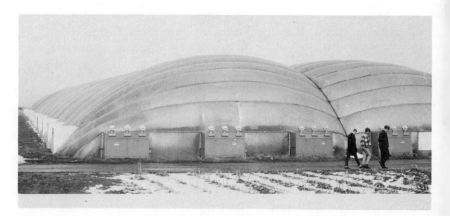

Figure 62. *The inflated plastic bubble greenhouse. This structure covers approximately one acre.* (ENVIRONMENTAL STRUCTURES, INC., CLEVELAND AND SMITH-VILLE, OHIO).

Arizona in Tucson (Fig. 64). Others consist of rigid vertical fiberglass sidewalls and a double layer plastic roof. A positive air pressure maintained between the two plastic sheets provides a dead air space of varying depths (Fig. 43).

The advantages and disadvantages associated with producing tomatoes under glass rather than plastic, fiberglass or PVC (polyvinyl chloride) may be summarized as follows. Transmitted light is probably superior in plastic and fiberglass greenhouses because it is more diffused and there are fewer structural barriers. Fiberglass, PVC, and especially plastic greenhouses, are essentially air tight. This characteristic makes carbon dioxide enrichment, fumigation, and heating, especially in double-layer plastic houses with air between the layers, more economical. On the other hand, the demands for ventilation, air circulation, temperature control, and air exchange are more critical. Controlling the fungus diseases that affect

Figure 63. *Lettuce production inside the plastic bubble. Note the lack of internal supports and tie-downs.*

Figure 64. *Air-inflated low-cost greenhouses. University of Arizona installations at Puerto Peñasco, Sonora, Mexico.*

tomato foliage is more difficult in plastic, PVC, and fiberglass struc-tures. The most prevalent and serious fungus disease during the late fall, winter, and early spring is gray mold (*Botrytis cineria*), which thrives at low (below 65°F) temperatures. Late blight (*Phytophthora infestans*) can also occur at low temperatures. Early blight (*Alternaria solani*) requires high temperatures. Leaf mold (*Cladosporium ful-vum*) flourishes under warm (65 to 75°F), humid (above ninety-five percent relative humidity) conditions. It is the most destructive disease that affects greenhouse-grown tomatoes in May and June and during the fall. Control of these fungus diseases, a prerequisite for successfully producing tomatoes in plastic greenhouses, is the most important production challenge that must be met.

The comparative heat requirements of double- and single-layer plastic and glass greenhouses have been determined (Table 31). B.T.U. values are based on one thousand square feet of exposed surface and the difference between inside and outside temperatures. A double-layer plastic greenhouse requires only five-eighths as much heat as a glass structure to maintain a given temperature, and con-serves heat far more efficiently than a singlelayer plastic house. Other

TABLE 31. Comparative heat in BTU's required per 1000 sq. ft. of exposed surface in different types of greenhouses and according to differences between outside and inside temperatures (After D. J. Cotter and J. M. Walker, University of Kentucky, Lexington, Kentucky 40506).

Temperature difference (°F)	Plastic		Glass
	Double layer	Single layer	
	(thousands of BTU's)		
40	28	50	45.2
50	35	62.5	56.5
60	42	75	67.8
70	50	87.5	79.1

energy conservation practices relating to greenhouse structures and materials will be covered under the section to follow on Energy and Heating Economy.

ஜ PLASTIC HOUSES FOR FALL AND SPRING CROPS

Many of the practices recommended for the successful production of tomatoes in glass greenhouses can also be used for plants grown in plastic greenhouses. While permanent glass installations are superior to temporary plastic, excellent spring and fall tomato crops can be grown in either temporary or more permanent plastic structures. As indicated above, most plastic films present no serious barrier to sunlight transmission and may be advantageous, even when two layer covers are used.

In addition to the low cost of the initial construction and of the heating, using plastic greenhouses for tomato production allows the grower to seed fall crops in late June. The plants can then be set in rows and trained in the open frame until night temperatures fall below 60°F when the plastic sides and roof are put on. Such crops are not exposed to the excessively high temperatures that prevail within glass greenhouses during the late summer months. These high temperatures often result in widespread crop failures, a difficulty experienced by many growers in the fall of 1959.

Figure 65. *These large closely spaced fruit clusters were produced on a fall crop by transplanting the plants in an open frame in mid-August and covering with plastic in late September. Experimental fall planting, Michigan State University, November 7, 1958.*

Vigorous, thick-stemmed plants are produced with closely spaced fruit clusters (Fig. 65). Flowers are pollinated by the prevailing outdoor winds. The usual problems with leaf mold on a fall crop are also bypassed, at least until the frame is covered with plastic. Yields of six to eight pounds of marketable fruit per plant (Table 32) have been obtained in experimental fall plantings which were started in open frames and later covered with plastic at the approach of the first frost and freezing temperatures. However, leaving greenhouses uncovered until late summer or early fall may be hazardous, as this practice allows for the free passage of aphids and other insects and the transmission of virus diseases into the crop.

High yielding (eighteen to twenty-two pounds of fruit per plant at a density of 10,000 plants per acre) spring crops of tomatoes may be produced in properly constructed and managed plastic greenhouses (Table 33). Plants may be set as early as February 15 in the northern areas of the United States. In less refined plastic greenhouses with heating and ventilating problems, crops should be timed to mature

TABLE 32. Comparative fall crop (1958) yields of Michigan–Ohio Hybrid and Ohio WR–7 Globe tomatoes grown in plastic and glass greenhouses.

Cluster No.	Plastic greenhouse		Glass greenhouse	
	M–O Hybrid	WR–7 Globe	M–O Hybrid	WR–7 Globe
	(pounds of marketable fruit harvested on each plant)			
1	1.7	1.4	1.7	1.1
2	2.3	1.9	1.5	1.4
3	1.3	1.5	1.5	1.5
4	1.2	1.3	1.3	0.9
5	0.9	0.9	1.7	1.7
Total yields (lbs./plant)	7.4	7.0	7.7	6.6

fruit only four to six weeks before locally grown outdoor tomatoes become available. Plants for such a crop are set in ground beds between March 15 and April 1.

Fruit of this late spring crop should begin to ripen by May 25 or June 1. Shortly thereafter, the plastic or sections of it could be removed. As with fall crops, ventilation, disease control, and pollination may be greatly simplified during part of the growth and fruiting period by partially or completely removing the plastic.

ईस ENERGY AND HEATING ECONOMY

◎ *Solar Energy.* A greenhouse can be an excellent solar energy collector. This may be either an asset or a liability. In the summer excess heat must be removed, and in the winter it may be a source of supplementary heat during periods of sunlight. The structural design of a greenhouse can be modified to improve its solar energy collection and heat retention potential (Fig. 66). Solar energy engineers are also designing equipment to store solar heat and use it when required. Periods when day and night temperature differentials are great—such as during fall and spring months—provide the best opportunity to use such a system to economize in heating costs.

TABLE 33. Marketable yields of greenhouse tomatoes grown by ring and trough culture in plastic greenhouses, Spring, 1967.[a] (Courtesy of Dr. Merle Jensen, Rutgers, the State University, New Brunswick, New Jersey 08903.)

Type of culture	Variety	Total marketable yield	
		Lbs./plant	Tons/acre
Ring	Michigan–Ohio Hybrid	21.2	106
	Veegan	21.4	107
	Tuckcross–0	21.8	109
Trough	Michigan–Ohio Hybrid	18.2	91
	Veegan	21.5	108
	Tuckcross–0	21.5	108

[a] Plants were set in the greenhouse February 15, at a density of 10,000 plants per acre; harvest began May 2 and continued until July 28. The floor of the greenhouse was covered with opaque white plastic for greater light reflection. Seedlings were given the cold treatment, and other practices outlined in this book were followed.

Figure 66. *A solar A-frame type greenhouse designed for northern climates. Cool season crops (lettuce, radishes, spinach) were grown throughout the 1977–1978 winter months. Tomatoes required supplementary heat.* (DESIGNED BY REED A. MAES, ENVIRONMENTAL RESEARCH INSTITUTE OF MICHIGAN, ANN ARBOR, MI 48107).

Early experiments in the storage of solar energy used water tanks and rock beds. Research on storage of "latent" heat is under way, and may lead to reductions in storage equipment and greater flexibility in system design. Stored energy will aid, but cannot be relied upon as the exclusive source of energy to heat a greenhouse during winter months, except for cool season crops such as lettuce.

Concurrently, trapping of solar energy is much more efficient by use of solar collectors than by a greenhouse. Such collectors could be on roofs of adjoining buildings, or on the ground outside the greenhouse area. Solar collectors have been developed for water and for air heating so that they could be used with existing greenhouse hot water and hot air systems.

The heat storage reservoir must maintain water temperatures higher than 50°F. The water is circulated from the reservoir during the day through the collectors or through the greenhouses so that temperature of the water is built up. When needed, the heated water is circulated through a heat exchanger to provide heat in the greenhouse. The size of the reservoir must be calculated according to the area to be heated and the rate of circulation of the water. When the temperature of the reservoir cannot be raised to the desired temperature, which is dependent on the total solar radiation for the day, the reservoir must be heated by use of conventional boilers. In such instances, the heat obtained from solar radiation would not be lost, since less fossil fuel would be needed to raise the water to the desired temperature.

Full use of solar energy for greenhouse heating in the future can come only if advantage is taken of the research conducted by solar energy engineers. This will involve studies of thermal characteristics of glass and plastics, their heat transfer, and use of absorbing surface coatings so that maximum collecting of energy can be achieved. [22] Additional knowledge is needed on the distribution of solar radiation as determined by the optimum shape and orientation of greenhouses and possible use of supplementary solar collectors and reflectors.

⊛ *Fuel Energy.* Energy conservation and resultant savings in heating costs are of great concern to the greenhouse tomato grower. There is hope that heat engineers will present new ideas for saving

[22] Proceedings Solar Energy—Fuel and Food Workshop, Environmental Research Laboratory, Tucson, Arizona. 1976.

heat and suggest alternative less costly heating systems. Greenhouses are heated with gas, oil, or coal. Although the efficiency of the modern heating plant is high, regular checks on fuel combustion are necessary for efficient operation. For gas and oil operated units, carbon dioxide concentrations and temperatures of flue gases must be properly monitored. A deposit of $\frac{1}{8}$ inch depth of soot on the boiler heating surface can increase the use of fuel up to 10 percent.

Fuel energy can be reduced by avoiding frequent starting and stopping of the boiler resulting from small differentials of the controls. Starting and stopping purges air into the boiler and is a source of heat loss. Where the return of condensate enters into an open uninsulated feed water holding tank, covering and insulation would retain the heat and reduce fuel usage. Each 11 degrees F rise in feed water of the boiler requires 1% more fuel. Other losses of heat may be mechanical, such as faulty steam traps, loose flange connections, improperly packed valves, and poorly insulated steam lines.

Structural loss of heat, especially through glass, is extremely high. Thirty-eight percent of the fuel can be saved by double glazing. The greatest loss is from the roof of the house. The disadvantages of double glazing are the high cost and the reduced light transmission which may be as high as 14 percent, especially during the winter months when the lowest light intensity is experienced. Double glazing, while giving the greatest saving of heat in mid-winter, will result in a loss of light that could mean a greater dollar loss from the crop than the fuel saved. The use of liquid based foams injected between layers of polyethylene covering during the night has been investigated. The foam condenses to a liquid during the day and is stored. It is pumped and refoamed at night. This maximizes the daytime solar radiation collection and minimizes the loss of heat at night.

Two layers of polyethylene [23] on glasshouses have been used to reduce heat loss (Fig. 67) as much as 60 percent. The inflated covering will allow for light snowfall to slide down to the gutter and melt. Heavy snowfalls, however, may cause the covering to collapse, and the plastic touching the glass will increase the melting of snow. The disadvantage of placing an insulating cover over the glasshouses, whether inside or out, is that light transmission to the plants is reduced. For each percent of light reduction, there is a comparable percent loss in yield. In addition to the added cost, there are other

[23] Monsanto 602, 6 mil. Monsanto Chemical Co., St. Louis, Missouri.

Figure 67. *Two layers of polyethylene over glass with an inflated air space between the two film layers will reduce heat losses in midwinter by 60 percent.* (CLEVELAND, OHIO. WINTER *1978*).

problems with double layer plastic over glass greenhouses. Carbon dioxide should be added, humidity is increased, snow accumulates in the gutters and will not melt, repairs are difficult, and dirt gathers under the plastic. Double layer plastic over glass is best only on the north half of greenhouses that run east and west. It could be on both sides of greenhouses that run north and south.

Sealing of houses to save fuel may aggravate disease problems and increase sulfur dioxide, nitric oxide, and nitrogen oxide injury to crops where carbon dioxide enrichment is used. Sealing of houses to save fuel restricts ventilation and lessens air exchange. Where propane or oil burners are used for carbon dioxide enrichment, the accompanying decrease in ventilation may mean less ozone and less spare oxygen atoms to form nitrogen oxide which is less toxic than nitric oxide. Nitrogen and sulfur oxides cause tissue damage and foliar injury. Nitric oxide at 0.4 ppm may reduce photosynthesis and plant growth by as much as 30 percent.

Photoperiod blinds such as blackout or shading systems, or the thermal screens installed at night inside the house may result in fuel savings of 20 to 50 percent, depending on the type of material used from black polyethylene to aluminized polyester. The installation of such screens may be justified even if it is only operable at night.

The use of clear polyethylene as an internal or external lining on the windward side of the house has been practiced and is highly recommended to reduce the heat loss (Fig. 68). Heat losses from a normal greenhouse doubles as the wind speed increases from 0 to 20 miles per hour.

It has been calculated that 3–6 percent savings in fuel can be realized if the house is protected from the prevailing winds only, and 10 percent if the house can be protected all around. Erection of artificial screen or shelter belts on the windward side to reduce wind speed has also been suggested. Such shelters should be as high as the ridge of the house, 50 percent permeable and located at a distance of 10 times the height of the house.

Sealing of glass, including the aluminum glazing caps and areas around the gutter, as well as insulating the metal gutter, can reduce heat losses. Other structures such as poorly fitted ventilators, doors, and cracked or broken glass should be repaired or replaced to conserve heat.

Figure 68. *Polyethylene film as an external lining on the windward side of a glass greenhouse is highly recommended to reduce heat losses.* (THOMAS WOLFE GREENHOUSES, CLEVELAND, OHIO).

A new type of polyethylene (Infrane) film that has greater heat retention properties has been reported in Europe. The film provides a barrier to the escape of infra-red waves. This retains 84 percent of soil heat (infra-red), as compared to ordinary polyethylene which retains only 45 percent under similar conditions.

Setting a thermostat so that the air temperature is more than intended will greatly increase fuel consumption. It has been estimated that if the temperature is set at only 2 degrees more than intended, fuel consumption will increase by 18 to 25 percent for the heating season. As a rule, each degree increase in temperature means an increase in fuel use of 7 to 10 percent for temperatures ranging between 55 and 65°F. Control of air temperature requires a reliable and responsive thermostat. The money saved in the accuracy of the control far outweighs the cost of the instrument. The thermostat should be located at or near the level of the growing crop, away from doorways or other drafty areas, and in a properly aspirated shelter so that a representative sample of air reaches the instrument.

Delayed planting into permanent beds until the first flowers open will reduce the area occupied for growing which not only reduces fuel consumption, but increases the setting of the bottom cluster. Other methods for fuel saving are the lowering of night temperatures 4 degrees and comparable boosting of daytime temperatures. Increased yields have been reported by appropriate use of solar energy and higher temperatures during the light period. This can be done by using a light dependent control system and ventilating at 80° rather than 75. It has also been suggested that CO_2 enrichment should be extended with the delayed ventilation. These modifications in temperature will save fuel. Varieties that will respond most favorably, however, should be identified.

It would be unwise for growers of early tomatoes to shift to a later planted crop to reduce fuel requirements. Such a move would result in loss of the early market and reduce the possibility of keeping the cost per unit low by less than optimal use of the greenhouse. A few tons of high priced early fruit would help achieve this goal. A shift to later plantings would likely result in an over supply at mid-season with lower prices that would not compensate for the savings in fuel.

Other hazards resulting from a reduction in fuel use may be an increase in loss from diseases. With lower temperatures, there is a build-up of humidity. Increased humidity results if temperatures are reduced and vents kept closed for longer periods. This invites increased severity of leaf, stem, and fruit diseases. Interrelationships of humidity and temperature relate to the infectivity of fungal diseases. Fuel savings resulting from less than efficient steam sterilization may easily result in a higher incidence of disease. Too much is at stake to skimp on this important practice to save fuel.

ࣿ NEW TYPES OF CULTURE

Several growing techniques which originated in western Europe have been recently promoted to eliminate or reduce the need for steam sterilizing entire ground beds in greenhouses. These include using grafted plants and ring, trough, straw bale, peat module, rock wool, hydroponic culture, and the nutrient film technique. The principles involved are utilizing growing media other than soil and confining the root system in a relatively small volume. The chief advantage is increased productivity. Soil sterilization is also by-passed. The disadvantages are the extra cost and, at times, an increased labor requirement. Their place in greenhouse tomato culture in North America should receive serious consideration irrespective of the uncertainties and increasing costs of labor. In the United States, only a few small growers have thus far adopted these techniques. Brief descriptions of each follow.

    ◉   *Use of Grafted Plants.* Related tomato species which are resistant to root diseases have been used as rootstocks for grafted tomato plants in western Europe for a number of years. In the United States, a small number of growers are now using similar methods. Grafting is widely used by the Japanese in the production of greenhouse cucumbers and melons. Tomato plants used for rootstocks are normally started five to ten days earlier since the rootstock grows more slowly than the grafted scion variety. It is desirable for the stock and scion to be of equal size both in height and stem thickness. Every effort should be made to grow plants that are four to five inches tall with a stem diameter of one-fourth inch, since this is the best size for grafting.

    The grafting procedure is as follows. The plants are carefully removed from the soil. The top of the rootstock except for one or two leaves is removed. A downward cut is made on the rootstock; an upward cut on the scion variety. The lips are pushed into each other and wrapping material such as transparent adhesive tape is used to hold them together. The grafted plants are planted in a pot. A normal growing procedure is then followed.

◉ *Ring Culture.* This method of culture was widely used during the 1960's in western Europe. It has now been largely replaced by other systems. The tomato plant is set into a bottomless round (eight to ten inch diameter) ring or sleeve of plastic film or roofing paper. The rounds or containers are spread out (Fig. 69) in a bed of aggregate varying in depth from four to six inches.

Ring culture was originally promoted because it allows the tomato plant to form two separate root systems. The top root system is in a nutrient-absorbing medium and in a bottomless ring of soil or compost. The other is in an underlying medium of water-absorbing material (aggregate) largely devoid of nutrients except for some calcium, magnesium, and phosphorus. Ring culture is sometimes called the "two-zone" system. It is claimed that by planting in sawdust, compost or artificial mix and allowing the roots free access into a water-charged underlayer, the combined advantages of soil culture and hydroculture may be realized.

The "two-root zone" system of ring culture developed in western Europe has been modified.[24] Rather than running water with few, if any, nutrients in the lower level aggregate bed and fertilizers in the upper level or the sleeve or ring containers, the same materials (sphagnum peat moss, peat, vermiculite, sawdust, perlite) are used in both.

One of the major goals of ring culture is to produce greenhouse-grown tomatoes without the hazard of soil-borne disease-producing organisms. Accordingly, the underlying aggregate bed should be prepared at about a four-inch depth from sterile nontoxic materials which promote good rooting and aeration and have a high water-holding capacity. Fifty-fifty mixtures of sphagnum peat moss and vermiculite or peat and perlite are very effective. Superphosphate (eighteen to twenty percent) should be added at the rate of fifty pounds per thousand square feet and dolomitic (calcium-magnesium) limestone at the rate of one hundred pounds per thousand square

24 After Dr. Raymond Sheldrake, Cornell University, Ithaca, New York 14850.

Figure 69. *Ring culture.* (PHOTO COURTESY DR. R. SHELDRAKE, JR,. DEPARTMENT OF VEGETABLE CROPS, CORNELL UNIVERSITY, ITHACA, NEW YORK, 14850).

feet. The growing medium in the ring should also be prepared from similar sterile materials or from steam-sterilized soil mixes. After plants are set in the rings, starter fertilizer solutions high in phosphorus should be used; water and fertilizer should be added thereafter as needed.

If a liquid-feed system is used for ring culture, a constant supply of dilute fertilizer solution is injected into the water with each irrigation. This system makes it necessary for the grower to prepare the fertilizer each time the plants are irrigated and also to service the equipment. To circumvent these problems, the use of one application of slow release fertilizer that furnishes the total nutrient requirement for the entire crop has been suggested.[24] This is accomplished by adding to each cubic yard of the basic 1:1 sphagnum peat and vermiculite mixture the following materials: ground dolomitic limestone (12 pounds), gypsum (5 pounds), calcium nitrate (1.5 pounds), 20 percent superphosphate (2.5 pounds), iron (chelated NaFe 138) (1 ounce), and fritted trace elements (FTE 503) (3 ounces). Slow release plastic coated granular fertilizer such as

[24] After Dr. Raymond Sheldrake, Cornell University, Ithaca, New York 14850.

Osmocote and MagAmp are used to supply the season's requirement (spring and fall crops) of nitrogen, phosphorus, potassium, and magnesium. The use of either 7 or 14 pounds of Osmocote (14–14–14) and 12.3 pounds of 11–27–10, plus MagAmp 7–40–6, per cubic yard of the artificial mixture gives yields equal to or higher than the continuous liquid feed system.

⊛ *Trough Culture.* In this system, which originated on the Isle of Guernsey in the early 1960's, greenhouse tomatoes are grown in long, narrow plastic-lined beds containing a lightweight artificial root medium. The growing medium may contain sawdust, sphagnum peat, peat other than sphagnum, sand, perlite, vermiculite, or many combinations of these ingredients. The trough must be impermeable to roots.

Trough culture has many advantages. The operator has complete control of the growing medium which can be brought to the desired texture, pH and fertilizer level. Drainage and soil moisture may be completely regulated and controlled. Steam sterilization can be efficiently conducted. Soil-borne disease such as *Verticillium, Fusarium,* and bacterial wilts may be eliminated, since roots cannot penetrate into unsteamed paths or a subsoil. The incidence of tobacco mosaic virus is also reduced. Since the troughs, as well as the growing medium, can be standardized, all areas in all houses can be managed alike. Troughs filled with an aggregate rather than one of the above media are frequently used in hydroponic culture.

Troughs may be prepared with 1½ to 2-inch concrete slabs, ordinary concrete blocks (Fig. 70), or 1 x 6 or 2 x 6 inch lumber. Troughs should be five to six inches deep and the inside about twenty-four or more inches wide to accommodate two rows of tomatoes. The troughs are lined with four mil polyethylene or polyvinyl chloride plastic. Plants may be set from twelve to sixteen inches apart in each row; the rows should be from twelve to twenty-four inches apart, depending on the width of the trough.

The great disadvantage in trough culture is the initial cost of constructing and maintaining the troughs. Because of the need for more frequent irrigation, labor costs may also be higher, unless an automatic drip system is installed. In trough culture, water soluble fertilizers are usually added with each irrigation.

⊛ *Peat Culture.* The advantages of this culture are the conservation of energy in that soil sterilization is circumvented, and there is a faster turn around between crops. It is extensively used in England, Scandinavia, Holland, and the Isle of Guernsey. This type of culture has been particularly successful for replacing soil cultures that are difficult to manage or are borderline for greenhouse culture. The system utilizes small volumes of peat substrate that is isolated from the soil (Fig. 26, 74). Sphagnum peat is the basic material for the preparation of the substrate. A standard nutrient mix for preparing peat for troughs and modules is given in Table 34. The peat and fertilizer are thoroughly mixed, using a mechanical mixer with water added to moisten the mix. This substrate may be used in troughs, basin techniques, rings, mattresses, bags, bolsters, and modules.

With the peat mattress system, the prepared sphagnum peat is placed in a 2½ feet wide and 4–5 inch deep trough lined with a heavy black polyethylene plastic. A slight depression in the center of the trough is sloped along its length so it drains to one or both ends. The peat must be uniformly moist prior to planting. The plants should be set one inch above the plastic lining.

In the peat bolster method, the peat substrate is spread along a 2 foot wide polyethylene sheet, and the two long edges are folded over the peat substrate and stapled. Slits are made at the desired

Figure 70. *Trough culture. Concrete blocks may be used in preparing the troughs.* (A. W. MARSH, ROCKWOOD, MICHIGAN *48173*).

distance on this tube for setting the plants. Approximately $\frac{1}{2}$ cubic foot of substrate is allowed for each tomato plant.

With the peat bag system, $\frac{1}{2}$ cubic foot of peat is placed in a polyethylene bag and one plant is set in it. Lesser amounts of peat are used and the bag is perforated at the bottom, if a capillary matting technique is used for irrigation. In all of the above systems, irrigation and fertilization are through drip hoses or seep hoses if the bed surface is level. Fertilization formulations for the liquid feed are similar to that of hydroponic culture.

Prior recommendations as to use of grow bags were to thoroughly soak the peat before placing the plants in the medium and cutting slits in the bottom of the bag soon thereafter for drainage. This system causes young plants to grow rapidly, thus losing the first fruit cluster. To avoid this loss, plants with the first cluster already set are planted in the bags with the watering tube next to them. The dripping water will thoroughly wet the peat in the bag after which slits are made in the bottom for drainage.

Peat modules are used extensively on the Isle of Guernsey and in Great Britain. Their origin was in Finland. They are made of 14″ x 40″ plastic bags filled with 1.5 cubic feet of peat mix and heat sealed. The module will support three plants. Use of the module facilitates rapid changeover between plants. Substantial increases in productivity have been achieved with its use (Table 30). The greenhouse bed is first covered with a white plastic sheet to reflect light. The peat modules are then placed in rows at the plant density desired (Fig. 27, 71). Peat modules that will support two plants are under trial in the United States (Fig. 72).

Transplants showing flower buds ready to open are planted in the modules by removing a disc of plastic, or by cutting out a flap to expose the peat. The plant should not be planted more than one inch below the top of the pot.

Three to four weeks after planting the standard liquid fertilizer shown in Table 23 is fed to the plants. Once the peat substrate in the bag is thoroughly wet, drainage slits are made about one inch above the ground on the sides or ends of each bag.

The watering and feeding of the crop is similar to a soil-grown tomato crop. A drip or trickle system of watering should be used. The liquid feeding program should be dependent on the amount of sunlight and the stage of development of the crop. To avoid blossom-end rot, irrigate frequently with small amounts of water

Figure 71. *Peat modules. These consist of plastic bags of sphagnum peat each of which will support 3 plants.* (VAN HEYNINGEN BROS., LTD. NURSERIES, LITTLE-HAMPTON, ENGLAND).

Figure 72. *Peat modules. These consist of plastic bags of peat each of which will support 2 plants.* (AL GERHART GREENHOUSES, NORTH RIDGEVILLE, OHIO).

Figure 73. *Rockwool culture. The system utilizes mats of rockwool (3" x 12" x 35") that are isolated from the soil or floor by plastic sheets. Samples are being drawn from the rockwool to test the salinity.*

3–4 times daily. Regular chemical analysis (3–4 week intervals) of the peat substrate should be made to adjust fertilization of the crop.

The growing of the tomato crop in a restricted volume of peat requires a higher standard of management and skill than one grown in the soil. The margin of error in fertilizing and watering, however, is reduced with peat culture. The main disadvantage of the peat module is that it is presently not economical to re-use after one year because of cost of sterilizing, re-fertilizing, bagging, and moving of the material. Where troughs are used, the substrate could be sterilized in the trough after each crop, and thereby reduce the cost of production.

Peat modules, as used in Great Britain, are imported largely from Finland. Peat is a non-renewable resource. Alternatives to this culture should be sought.

◉ *Rockwool Mats and Blocks.* Rockwool is a sterile homogeneous product manufactured by melting basalt and limestone at 1,500°C and spinning the molten rock into 0.005 mm fibers. The fibers are treated with resin before cooling so they are capable of absorbing water and have 97% air space. Rockwool has become a popular tomato and cucumber growing medium in Sweden, Denmark, and to a limited extent in Holland. Mats of rockwool 3 inches thick, 12 inches wide, and 35 inches long are laid on plastic end to end on the ground (Fig. 28, 73). The plastic is 12 inches wider than the mat, and the ends are folded on the side and on the mat and held in place by wooden pins inserted into the mat. Each pad supports 3 plants. In using the mats, they should be thoroughly saturated prior to use with the recommended fertilizer solution. The amount of solution applied is determined by some water emerging from the bottom of the mat.

Tomato plants grown on rockwool blocks or on porous compost are placed on the mats. The roots should be penetrating from the blocks at transplanting time to allow the roots to penetrate the mats. The placing of the blocks on the mats drains the blocks and forces the roots downward. Keeping the mats moist with the required nutrient medium is important.

Nutrients and water are supplied by drip tubes that are placed on the blocks. As in hydroponics, the growing of plants on rockwool requires a good control over nutrients and should be based on periodic analysis. The pH and salt concentration should be checked weekly by drawing water samples from the mats with a syringe and the conductivity values determined. A reading of 2.5 mmhos is recommended. The salt content of the irrigation water is adjusted to this reading by increasing or decreasing the fertilizer concentration. Irrigation frequency varies from 1–4 times a day, depending on the size and type of plant, the season of the year, and the growing conditions in the greenhouse.

Rockwool mats have been successfully used for three successive crops. At the end of the growing season, after the crops are removed, the mats are placed on their side to drain the water. For the next crop, the mat is turned over and the new plants placed on it.

⊛ *Formulas for Artificial Soils or Mixes.* Successful ring and trough culture demand the use of standardized artificial mixes instead of soil for the root growth medium. These artificial mixes are initially low in nutrients and are free from disease organisms, insects, nematodes, and toxic residues. Suggested formulas are lightweight and consist of 1:1 mixture of vermiculite or perlite with sphagnum peat. Each cubic yard of the mix should be prepared as in Table 35. The ingredients (sphagnum peat, vermiculite, perlite) do not require sterilization before use in growing media. Local peat or muck has given inconsistent results and may require steam sterilization.

Water soluble chemical fertilizers are added to these lightweight artificial mixes as needed during the growth of the crop. The most convenient method is to meter all soluble fertilizer solutions through the irrigation system. Dilutions are suggested in Table 23.

⊛ *Sand Culture.* The bed is composed of 12 inches of washed sand laid over a plastic liner. The bottom of the beds are sloped to the middle, and the length of the bed is sloped to one end of the house to provide proper drainage. A strip of 1¼ or 1½ inch PVC pipe sliced in half is laid on the bottom through the length of the bed prior to filling with sand. The beds are two feet wide and an alley or aisle is 2½ feet. The plants are spaced on an 18-inch and 6-inch pattern and planted 3 to 4 inches deep in the sand. The nutrients and water get to the plants by use of a trickle type irrigation system with holes every 4–6 inches apart. The system is automated, watering four times a day with varying intervals of 5 to 8 minutes each time. The nutrients are premixed in nutrient tanks and through the use of metering devices are monitored prior to entering the drip or trickle irrigation system.

⊛ *Sawdust Culture.* The sawdust or sawdust-sand mixture is placed in beds, plastic pots, or bags. The bottom of the plastic lined beds is sloped to provide drainage of excess water. Two-row beds

TABLE 34. A standard nutrient mix for preparing peat for troughs, modules, mattresses, etc.[25]

Materials	Rate per cu. yd. (lbs.)	(oz.)	Rate per cu. meter (kg.)	Nutrient Level (ppm)
Ground Chalk	7	—	4.2	—
Dolomite	5	—	3.0	326 Mg.
Single Superphosphate	8	—	4.75	370P
Ammonium Nitrate	—	12	0.45	150N
Sulphate of Potash	2	8	1.5	590K
Frit WM 255	—	10	0.4	—

[25] Provided by D. J. Beddal, Horticultural Advisory Officer, Kent ADAS, 50, New Dover, Canterbury, England.

TABLE 35. Formulas for artificial mixes.[24]

Materials	Amount for Each Cubic Yard
Shredded sphagnum peat	11 bushes or ½ cubic yard
Vermiculite (No. 2 or 3)	11 bushes or ½ cubic yard
Finely ground limestone	10 pounds
Superphosphate (20%)	2 pounds
Calcium and Potassium nitrates	½ pound each
Iron chelate	1 ounce (1 tablespoon)
Fritted trace elements—	
F.T.E. 503	3 ounces

[24] Modified after Dr. Raymond Sheldrake, Cornell University, Ithaca, New York 14850. The fritted trace elements (F.T.E. 503) are available from the Ferro Corporation, 4150 E. 56th Street, Cleveland, Ohio 44105. If this product is not available, use ½ oz. of sodium borate (Borax) per cubic yard.

6–8 inches deep and providing ⅓ cubic foot of medium per plant are suggested. Movement of moisture laterally is better with the sawdust-sand mixture than sawdust alone, although with proper establishment of plants, sawdust could be used. Moderately fine sawdust with a good portion of plane shavings provide better moisture movement than coarse sawdust alone. Certain types of sawdust such as the Western red cedar should not be used, since they are toxic. Nutrients and water are distributed by use of a drip-hose or other types of trickle irrigation. Fertilizer is provided to the plants either by supplying a complete nutrient solution each day, or by mixing the nutrients with the medium prior to planting. The following amounts are added per cubic foot of sawdust: 2.4 ounces of superphosphate, 4 ounces of dolomitic limestone and minor elements. With this method, potassium nitrate and ammonium nitrate are applied through the season in a nutrient solution through the irrigation system. If the sawdust is to be used for the fall crop, only ½ of the pre-mix fertilizer and minor elements used for the spring crop are suggested.

For all the above special types of tomato culture, the water and nutrients are distributed through a thin capillary tube or through a "Drip-Hose." In the capillary tube system, a rigid plastic hose is laid between each double row from which a fine feeding tube (.045 inch inside diameter) is inserted for each plant. The ends of the feeding tubes are lead weighted, or 1 inch length of ½ inch hose or other means is used to anchor them (Fig. 74). The "Drip-Hose"

Figure 74. *Feeding tubes in the drip irrigation system for greenhouse tomatoes. One is provided for each plant and anchored into place.*

or twin-wall hose system is laid parallel one foot apart in the trough. The "Drip-Hose" with pores every 8 inches distributes the liquid uniformly.

The chief disadvantage of the above cultures is the extra labor required in growing the crop and the high initial costs of the materials and installations. Furthermore, most artificial mixes and cultures must be replaced after each crop or growing season. The great advantages reside in savings in fuel by not steam sterilizing, disease control, and the potential for precise management of moisture and nutrient levels resulting in potentially higher yields and better fruit quality. Growers in the U.S. should seriously consider adopting some of these new culture techniques.

◎   *Straw-Bale Culture.* In this system, greenhouse tomatoes are grown on top of decomposing bales of straw (Fig. 75). Water and then water and fertilizer are added before the plants are set. The method, which originated in western Europe in the early 1960's, is now widely used in growing cucumbers and, to a lesser extent, tomatoes. Several growers in the United States have successfully

Figure 75. *Straw-bale culture of greenhouse tomatoes, illustrating different stages in the growth and fruiting of the plants for a fall crop. Left to right; September, October and November 1968.* (COURTESY, JIM ELLISON, RESEARCH FARMS, P.O. BOX *14604*, HOUSTON, TEXAS *77021*).

utilized this technique for tomatoes. Others have followed in a limited way for both fall and spring crops. Straw-bale culture has been used successfully in greenhouses with disease ridden soils which are not fumigated or those which may be chemically contaminated.

The essentials of straw-bale culture are as follows. Two to three thousand bales (forty to seventy-five tons) of wheat, barley, or oat straw are required per acre. The exact amount depends on the length and size of the bales and width of the rows. Like ring and trough culture, the goal of straw-bale culture is to circumvent soil sterilization and reduce losses from soil-borne pathogens. A sheet of four mil plastic (polyethylene), a foot wider on each side than the width of the bale, is first placed on the ground with approximately five-foot centers along the length or width of the house allowed for row spacing. The bales are then placed on the plastic with the ties up to avoid puncturing the film.

Fifteen to twenty days before setting the plants, the bales are thoroughly wetted. This is best done by several waterings spaced over two to three days. Fermentation or decomposition of the straw is next induced by adding nitrogen at the rate of forty pounds of ammonium nitrate per ton of straw (approximately three-fourths pound per bale). Three to five days later, additional fertilizer is added, consisting of twenty pounds each of di-ammonium phosphate, potassium nitrate, and calcium nitrate, plus seven pounds of magnesium sulfate with micronutrients as needed. A suggested procedure for watering the bales is to use the amounts of fertilizer indicated above for each thousand gallons of water added. A liquid proportioner could be used. After these additions of fertilizer and water, decomposition proceeds rapidly, with temperatures in the center of the bales reaching 110 to 130°F.

The tomato plants can be transplanted onto the bales after the temperature drops below 100°F. A single line of plants is set on the bales with alternate plants inclined outwards to the left and the right to form a double row. Crop management thereafter is comparable to conventional soil culture with two exceptions. Twine should be attached loosely to the vines with some slack to prevent the roots from being pulled out of the bales as the straw settles, and the water requirement is greater because of the larger evaporative surface from the straw. All soluble fertilizers are added as needed, preferably through the irrigation system. Additional assets of straw culture in greenhouse tomato production reside in the temperatures generated by the fermentation of the straw plus the carbon dioxide released which may greatly benefit early growth. Again, as with ring and trough culture, disadvantages are the extra labor and costs. Availability of straw may also be a crucial factor.

⊚   *Hydroponic Culture.* Beginning in 1965, a tremendous enthusiasm was generated for hydroponic culture through effective sales promotion. [26] A commercially sponsored symposium and conference on hydroponic culture of greenhouse tomatoes was held January 20–22, 1967 at Dallas, Texas. In the United States, there are an estimated three to five hundred hydroponic installations with a total of over two hundred acres (Fig. 7). Most of these are small units ranging from one-tenth to one-fourth acre, but there are a few one to three acre establishments (Fig. 76, 77).

Commercial hydroponic culture as it is now developing consists of a greenhouse designed to control the critical environmental factors

[26] First by Pan American Hydroponics, Inc., Route 3, Box 374, Grapevine, Texas; followed by Hydroculture, Inc., Glendale, Arizona; and more recently by Hygroponics, Inc., Panama City, Florida.

Figure 76. *Hydroponic culture. The essential components are beds or troughs, an aggregate, and a formulated nutrient solution pumped into the beds periodically. This is a one-third acre complex consisting of three houses 42' x 120' constructed at a cost of $55,000. 1968.* (BLAINE LUNDQUIST, MORGAN, UTAH).

Figure 77. *Commercial hydroponic culture.* (TOP, ROYAL GARDEN FARMS, INC., HURRICANE, UTAH, APRIL *1970;* BOTTOM, HYDROCULTURE, INC., GLENDALE, ARIZONA).

of air and root temperatures, relative humidity, air movement and circulation, carbon dioxide concentration in the atmosphere, mineral nutrient composition, pH of the water, intensity and duration of available sunlight, sterilization of the root-growing medium, and frequency of root-feeding cycles. Local aggregates are utilized for growing plants in specially designed tanks or beds. Irrigation is accomplished by an automated battery of pumps. There are regularly timed nutrient applications. The solution that drains off is returned to storage tanks and pumped back again during the next cycle. Nutrients are replenished in the storage tanks as needed or as revealed by periodic plant nutrient solution analyses.

Sensing devices have been developed that actuate the pumps on demand, rather than using time clocks. The sensor is controlled by the moisture in the growing medium at the root level. On a cloudy or rainy day, the plants may be fed only once or twice, whereas on a hot, dry, sunny day the sensor may call for several feedings.

There are several items that must be considered in the production of hydroponically grown tomatoes. These include water analysis, the growing medium, and the fertility level.

The most important ingredient is the type of water available. The water should be analyzed for the various elements, especially calcium and magnesium, so that the combined elements that are provided by the fertilizer and water do not exceed the established limit for the crop. Equally important, is the amount of salts that are in the water. The total salts from the fertilizer and water should not exceed 2500 parts per million (ppm). Commercial fertilizer used for hydroponic culture should have a dissolved salt content between 1000 and 2000 ppm. Although the pH of the water is not important in determining the above factors, the pH of the solution must be maintained at 6.0 to 6.5 with sulfuric or phosphoric acid.

Smooth, inert, $\frac{1}{4}$ to $\frac{3}{8}$-inch size gravel is the most popular medium used for hydroponic culture. The aggregate should be free of calcium carbonate or limestone. Gravel with higher than 5 percent calcium carbonate is not desirable, since it would precipitate certain elements necessary for growth and fruiting. One-fourth to $\frac{3}{8}$-inch size gravel allows the water and nutrients to move freely between the gravel, permits good drainage, and facilitates movement of oxygen to the plant roots.

Plants grown hydroponically do best when the solutions are properly balanced. The nutrients in the water and those supplied by the fertilizer should be in the desired range for the crop. Too much of one or more of the elements may have a toxic effect, while too little may cause deficiencies. The following approximates the ppm of an element in one ounce of fertilizer in 100 gallons of water: percent by weight of the element in the fertilizer x 75 = ppm.

The following nutrient formula [27] approximates the concentration in ppm of ions or elements needed for growing of tomatoes in the summer (long days and bright sunshine): nitrogen 200 ppm, phosphorus 53 ppm, sulfate 474 ppm, potassium 365 ppm, calcium 228 ppm and magnesium 47 ppm.

It is essential that the nutrient solution be analyzed every 2 days for nitrogen, and at least once a week for the other elements. It is also important to avoid high salts. Therefore, the solution should be regularly monitored. The tomato plant prior to fruit set could use the same solution for about three weeks. When the plants have a full load of fruits, weekly solution changes are recommended. Leaf petiole samples should be taken every 2 weeks so that a desirable nutrient level can be maintained for the growing of the crop (Tables 20, 21).

Formulas for hydroponic culture are many. No nutrient formula is superior to others. Many growers prefer to buy ready-mixed formulas, thus avoiding the labor and difficulties of mixing the various chemical ingredients. Listed below are examples of nutrient mixtures that have been used for the growing of tomatoes. The chemicals, both the major and minor nutrients, are mixed in large quantities in a concentrated form in solution. Availability of some of the nutrients is affected by the pH of the solution. For best results, the solution should be kept between a pH of 5.5 and 6.5. Since the buffering capacity of the solution is practically nil, the pH must be frequently monitored. Sulfuric acid is normally added to the solution to lower the pH.

The formulas are given in grams, since only small amounts of micronutrients are used. There are 28.35 grams to an ounce, and 473 milliliters to a pint. Difficulties in measuring small amounts of chemicals can be avoided by making a large batch of micronutrients and appropriate porportioning to obtain the proper formulation. Micronutrients are slow to dissolve in cold water, therefore, the use of hot water is suggested.

The following solution was developed in Texas. [28] It has given good results and eliminated the problem of macro and micronutrient deficiencies which have been noted for crops grown in the South. The ingredients and water should equal 100 gallons of solution.

[27] Suggested by John Larsen, Department of Horticulture, Texas A & M University, College Station, Texas.
[28] Obtained from John Larsen, Department of Horticulture, Texas A & M University, College Station, Texas.

Potassium nitrate	(13–0–44)	67 grams
Calcium nitrate	(15.5–0–0)	360 grams
Potassium magnesium sulfate	(0–0–22)	167 grams
Potassium sulfate	(0–0–50)	130 grams
Chelated iron	(Chel 330–10% Fe)	11.5 grams
Phosphoric acid	(75%)	50 milliliter
Manganese sulfate	(27% Mn)	1.5 grams
Boric acid		2.2 grams
Zinc sulfate	(36% Zn)	0.5 grams
Copper sulfate	(25% Cu)	0.5 grams
Molybdenum trioxide	(66% Mo)	0.04 grams

The micronutrient, manganese sulfate is doubled (3.0 grams) when the nutrient solution is used during the winter months (December to March).

The following nutrient formula has been suggested for young tomato plants in sand cultures using a drip irrigation system. [29] For older fruiting plants the amount of calcium nitrate is increased. Each time water is added to the sand, one gallon of stock solution is injected into each 200 gallons of water passing through the watering system, or the stock solution is measured in a large tank and pumped directly to the crop. If calcareous sand is used, the amount of chelated iron must be increased. Calcium nitrate is increased from 189.4 grams to 256.8 grams after the first fruit set to the end of the crop. The nutrients listed below, together with water, should equal 100 gallons of solution.

Magnesium sulfate	186.5 grams
Monopotassium phosphate	102.9 grams
Potassium nitrate	76.5 grams
Calcium nitrate	189.4 grams
Chelated iron	9.6 grams
Boric acid	1.0 grams
Manganous chloride	0.9 grams
Cupric chloride	0.05 grams
Molybdenum thioxide	0.02 grams
Zinc sulfate	0.15 grams

Another formula found satisfactory for hydroponically grown greenhouse tomatoes comes from Great Britain. [30] The major ele-

[29] Supplied by Merle H. Jensen, Environmental Research Laboratories, University of Arizona, Tucson International Airport, Tucson, Arizona 85706.
[30] Supplied by A. J. Cooper, Glasshouse Crops Research Institute, Littlehampton, Sussex, England.

ments should be dissolved in separate containers prior to adding to the circulation or injector tanks. The amount of all elements, including water, should again equal 100 gallons of solution.

Potassium nitrate	253.6 grams
Magnesium sulfate	177.9 grams
Calcium nitrate	374.7 grams
Potassium phosphate	52.9 grams
Iron sequestrine	6.9 grams
Manganese sulfate	0.8 grams
Boric acid	0.7 grams
Zinc sulfate	0.1 grams
Copper sulfate	0.1 grams
Ammonium molybdate	0.03 grams

Hydroponically grown tomatoes are comparable in quality and yield to those grown in soil culture. Any alleged superiority in flavor or color is slight and the result of more precisely controlled water and nutrient levels. Growers trained in the physiology of tomato plant growth and commercial production can achieve yields of fruit comparable to, and sometimes greater than, those grown in good soil or by other specialty cultures.

Hydroponic culture is a non-soil system of growing tomato plants. This in one sense is true also of ring, trough, bolster, peat modules, sawdust, rock wool, and straw bale culture. The difference, however, is that ring, trough, bolster, peat modules, sawdust, and straw bale cultures have built-in buffering systems which allow for greater flexibility in avoiding mineral starvation or toxicity. Automated pH control systems for hydroponic culture, however, have recently been designed. They enable growers to keep the pH of the nutrient solution constant and at any desired level.

Nutritional problems in hydroponic culture are especially difficult to identify. What appear to be deficiency symptoms, may, in reality, be toxicities. Regular mineral nutrient analyses of leaf tissues (Tables 20, 21), experienced interpretation of the results of such analyses, and the ability to relate the results to fertilizer applications and adjustments in the nutrient solutions are required.

The other obvious and compelling disadvantage of hydroponic culture is the high initial cost of materials and installation. These costs range from two hundred and fifty to eight hundred dollars per acre, well above that expended for greenhouses designed for conventional soil culture. A part of this initially greater investment

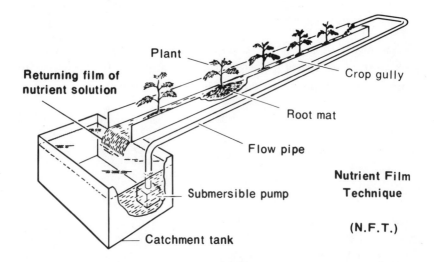

Plant

Returning film of
nutrient solution

Crop gully

Root mat

Flow pipe

Nutrient Film
Technique

Submersible pump

(N.F.T.)

Catchment tank

Figure 78. *The nutrient film technique. This system had its origin through the efforts of Dr. A. J. Cooper and associates of the Glasshouse Crops Research Institute, Littlehampton, England.* (PHOTOS COURTESY GLASSHOUSE CROPS RESEARCH INSTITUTE). *Top, diagrammatic outline; bottom, tomato plants as they appear in actual culture.*

may, however, be compensated for by greater automation and lower operating costs. Moreover, hydroponic culture makes it possible to increase the amount of light available to plants in winter. Walkways may be painted white (Fig. 77), and strips of opaque white plastic placed over the growing beds between the plant rows will reflect light back onto the plants. White plastic may also be placed between plant rows with conventional soil or peat module culture (Fig. 72, 73).

◎ *Nutrient Film Technique (NFT).* Perhaps the first real breakthrough in a completely automated feeding system in the production of greenhouse tomato crops is the nutrient film technique (NFT). This modified simple system of hydroponics research began in 1965 at the Glasshouse Crops Research Institute, Littlehampton, England. The term NFT was coined at the Glasshouse Crops Research Institute to emphasize that the depth of the liquid flowing in the tube was shallow—little more than a film. The film of nutrient flowing along the roots was at the bottom, the greater portion of the roots was in the air so that the roots were well supplied wih oxygen (Fig. 78). The NFT system is being tested in more than 60 countries, including the U.S. and Canada. The NFT system appeals to the grower because of its ease of installation, its adaptability to any type of protected house, and the reduction in time of changeover between crops. The old crop can be cut down and removed in a short time, the nutrient solution changed, the troughs flushed with formalin, and a new crop planted. Other advantages include being able to change the solution very quickly if anything goes wrong and the lack of need for tubes and nozzles which eliminates the blocking of feeder lines. For the grower who is building a new house, this system makes installation of an irrigation system unnecessary.

The NFT system for tomato production has the greatest potential in arid areas, since it eliminates the need for a large water storage facility. There is minimum evaporation loss, since the roots are confined in a closed system. Water is only lost through the plant's transpiration and, therefore, offers maximum water economy. The system may also be suited to hillsides facing south, or on rock or barren ground. Other advantages are precise control of the nutrient solution for optimum plant growth by proper monitoring and dosage equipment, and by maintenance of optimal root temperature (78°F) of the solution. No drainage loss and recirculation of the nutrient solution means less use of fertilizers; and savings in labor, fuel costs, and the elimination of soil-borne diseases. It also provides the opportunity for disease and pest control by application of systemic pesticides and fungicides into the NFT circulating system. Heating of the nutrient solution allows for the root zone to warm up, which prevents root wilting and enables the grower to run the houses at a lower air temperature. Use of a heated solution gives a better set of fruit on the lower tomato clusters and a better fruit grade.

The principle of the NFT is to confine the roots of tomato plants in a channel or gully that is made of an 18-inch black polyethylene film (1.5 ml) flume through which a shallow (1 millimeter) stream of nutrient solution is recirculated continuously by use of a pumping and gravity system (Fig. 78 top). In setting up the system, there is need for a two-way fall on the land. The catchment trench is dug across the middle or end of the bed which slopes to one end of the house. The bed is sloped to the trench from both ends so that the nutrient solution in the channel or gully will drain into the catchment gully or pipe which flows into the catchment tank. The trench and tank are lined with 4 ml black polyethylene film. The slope of the bed must be smooth to eliminate localized depressions with a minimum gradient of one inch in 100 feet. Localized depressions result in stagnant pools of nutrient solution which inhibit aeration and limit the necessary oxygen supply to the roots. The steeper the slope, the less careful need be the preparation of the slope of the bed to the catchment gully or pipe. The gully or channel is laid on an 8-inch wide hard board or on the smooth ground at normal plant row spacing.

The channels or gullies are prepared in two ways. In the first, polyethylene film is laid on the ground and rock wool cubes, 4½ inch whalehide pots, peat pots, Jiffy 7, or 2½ inch plastic mesh pots filled with artificial media are positioned in the middle of the film in a straight row. The sides of the film are turned up on the sides of the pot, soil block, or cube, and the edges stapled or clipped together at every other cube or pot. This forms a flat flume or gully to allow a shallow stream of nutrient solution to flow. The lower end of the channel is left hanging down in the catchment trench, while the upper end is sealed. The catchment trench is sloped so that the nutrient flows into the catchment tank. The nutrient solution in the catchment tank is pumped through flexible or rigid plastic pipe and is discharged from the flow pipe through small bore flexible discharge pipes into the channel or gully (Fig. 78 top).

Although the initial roots are confined to the growing media, the root develops in the nutrient solution. As mentioned earlier, it is important not to allow a depth of liquid to build up in the channels for, if only a film of solution flows through the channels, a thick mat of root develops above the film. This insures that all of the roots are moist, but the upper surface of the root mat is in the air. Algae do not seem to be a serious problem. The use of potted plants instead of bare rooted plants was found to be advantageous, since the pots served in the formation of the flume or gully and also provided a means of plant support in the early stages of growth, as well as facilitated the handling of the plants. Another advantage provided by this system was the rapid growth of seedlings over the conventional system resulting from the elimination of the drying cycle between waterings and the warm solution flowing in the channel or gully.

The second method calls for wooden stakes, approximately 4 inches high, to be placed in the ground at each end of the row. Two strands of fine wire are stretched between the stakes and twisted until taut. If the row is long, several stakes may be placed to hold the wire. The strip of black polyethylene film is laid next to the wire and the edges are clipped to the wire, using laundry clothes pins, forming a gully which allows the nutrient solution to flow freely (Fig. 78 bottom). The gully would appear triangular in cross section. The gully walls must be sufficiently closed to prevent algae growth and, at the same time, allowing sufficient ventilation and escape of undesirable gases such as ethylene. The plants are placed in the channel in pots, cubes, or blocks (Fig. 78 bottom).

Polyethylene channels are now being manufactured commercially in England and Italy. One form of gully holds the plants at the apex of the triangle allowing the use of bare rooted plants. Another is an extruded self supporting polyethylene gully "hydrocanal" which has a life span of 3–4 years in warmer countries and longer in England. The edges are fastened by use of studs. These studs provide a means of fastening or fixing support strings as well as the spacer piece of the stud providing for the exchanging of gases from the root system.

In England, the use of semi-rigid troughs with a life span of 5 years was found to be unsatisfactory, since they buckled badly from greenhouse heat. The use of black polyethylene with a life span of 3 years was preferred. It is also less expensive.

The nutrient solution is supplied through the inlet ends of the channels through a plastic flow pipe at right angle to the gullies. A 1/16 inch hole is made in the flow pipe at each gully and at an angle so the solution falls forward and downward into the gully. Alternatively, a small bore flexible discharge pipe is used from the flow pipe to the gully. The nutrient solution is either pumped from the catchment tank into the flow pipe, or flows by gravity from a header tank which is placed 5–6 feet high. The flow from the header tank is controlled by valves to insure even flow of the nutrient solution. The header tank is continually fed from the catchment tank. An overflow pipe from the header tank to the catchment tank allows for a direct return of the solution. A pump with sufficient capacity to insure that the overflow pipe has a continuous flow is used so that solution is above the valve controlling the water inlet of the header tank. The ends of the gully hang down into the catchment gutter, or an outlet pipe is connected to the large diameter flexible plastic catchment pipe which carries the liquid by gravity to the catchment tank. The gutter and catchment tank are covered to prevent algae growth. The supply of water to the catchment tank is controlled by a float valve to replenish water losses from the plants. As a guard against pump failure, a water valve is also installed about 1/3 from the bottom of the header tank so that if the nutrient solution level falls below the valve level, the valve will open and allow for a flow of water to enter the tank, providing a safeguard for the crop to survive until normal pumping could be restored. An overflow pipe in the catchment tank will allow for this water to go to waste. In such an event when normal pumping is restored, the diluted solution is disposed and fresh solution is used. The use of a flow sensor which trips an alarm if water is not passing over it is suggested. The alarm would sound if there is any interruption in electricity or pump failure. This instrument is placed in one of the gullies. Other forms of fail-safe devices are a duplicate pumping system, or a standby pump to cut in, in case the master pump fails, along with a standby electric generator and a reservoir of water if there is dependence upon an outside supply.

Long troughs should have inlets at 30 to 35 feet intervals. This arrangement will introduce fresh oxygen and nutrients at the inlet points. Where warm nutrient solution is used, it will compensate for temperature losses that occur over the length of the long row. The outlet point is the end of the trough into which the nutrient returns to the main tank.

Tomato plants grown in liquid flowing past their roots may have a greater tolerance to variations in nutrient concentration than when grown in soil. Concentrations at the inlet end of the gully are higher than at the discharge end of the gully, provided a continuous flow of even at the lower end of the gully, provided a continuous flow of nutrient is maintained. All greenhouse vegetables, and many other crops, respond equally well to the same nutrient solution in the NFT system. Hence, it may be practical to monitor the nutrient concentration by measuring the electrical conductivity of the solution, eliminating the necessity to analyze the individual elements. As the various elements are removed by the growing plant, the electrical conductivity decreases. If the cf (conductivity factor) falls below 20, nutrients are added to the catchment tank so that the cf is restored to 30. The level recommended for the tomato is cf 20 to 30. The use of automatic monitoring and dosage equipment would maintain a narrower range.

The pH of the solution is maintained between 6 and 7, and when the pH rises above 7, phosphoric or nitric acid is added. The rise in pH occurs as a result of removal of nutrients by the crop. Automatic equipment that continually monitors pH and cf and injects phosphoric or nitric acid and other nutrients to maintain programmed levels of nutrient and acidity is available in England. Manual portable battery operated equipment for checking pH and cf is also available. One can expect the probes to fail in the use of such instruments because of the acidity of the nutrient solution, where acid is pumped to lower the pH. Timers should be used for the acid and nutrient injection pumps to prevent excess dosages in case of instrument failure.

The nutrient solution (Table 36) as suggested by Dr. A. J. Cooper, of the Glasshouse Crops Research Institute in Littlehampton, Sussex, England, is reported suitable for most crops throughout the year and for most locations. Two formulations are suggested; the starting solution with which the catchment tank is filled at the beginning of the crop, and the topping up solution which is added when the nutrient solution in the catchment tank falls to a value of cf 20. A commercially formulated complete nutrient mix for NFT is available in England. It is important for NFT that ammonium nitrogen not be used in the solution, since it has an adverse effect on plant growth at lower concentrations.

Since the introduction of NFT, growers are seeking more facts.

TABLE 36. Nutrient solution formulations for the Nutrient Film Technique (NFT)

Salt	Formula	Starting Solution		Topping-up Solution	
		Wt of Salt gms/100 gals. H₂O	Conc. (ppm)	Weight of salt gms/100 gals. H₂O	Concentration (ppm)
Calcium nitrate	Ca(NO₃)₂.4 H₂O	374.2	117 (N) 168 (Ca)	149.6	47 (N) 67 (Ca)
Potassium nitrate	KNO₃	249.3	254 (K) 91 (N)	139.2	142 (K) 51 (N)
Magnesium Sulphate	MgSO₄.7 H₂O	188.1	49 (Mg)	122.8	32 (Mg)
Potassium phosphate	KH₂PO₄	103.0	62 (P) 78 (K)	—	—
Chelated Iron	FeNa EDTA	29.88	12 (Fe)	12.45	5 (Fe)
Manganous Sulphate	MnSO₄. H₂O	2.33	2 (Mn)	0.58	0.5 (Mn)
Boric Acid	H₃BO₃	0.649	0.3 (B)	0.649	0.3 (B)
Copper Sulphate	CuSO₄.5 H₂O	0.862	0.07 (Cu)	0.862	0.07 (Cu)
Ammonium molybdate	(NH₄)₆Mo₇O24.4 H₂0	0.035	0.05 (Mo)	0.035	0.05 (Mo)
Zinc sulphate	ZnSO₄.7 H₂O	0.014	0.07 (Zn)	0.014	0.07 (Zn)

Experiments, thus far, have been on a small scale, and the results used as a base for large scale production. There has also been concern as to the need for weekly analyses of the solution, as well as the pH of the water used in the system. The system requires precise management, speedy and detailed analyses of the nutrient solution, and proper interpretation. Failure to make the necessary corrections increases the probability of serious losses—not only of a few plants, but possibly the entire crop.

Little has yet been recorded concerning disease risks with NFT. If fungus spores get into the system, the nutrient solution and spores are circulated, and the entire area may be eventually infected. Crops infected with *Phytopthora* and *Colletotrichum* have poor root systems and low production. *Fusarium* and *Verticillium* wilts can also enter the system with devastating results. Good hygiene should be practiced with NFT as with other cultural methods. The houses and all equipment should be properly sterilized with 2 percent formalin between crops. The very latest indications suggest that disease will not pose any greater problem than now exists with conventional growing media.

Two plant problems, collar burn and root death, have been reported with this system. Collar burn consists of burnt-looking areas of the stem where it joins the liquid in the film channel caused by precipitation of salts at that region. This disorder seems to occur where the water is still or too deep, or where there are dead areas in the channel caused by a depression where only the top of the water flows as a current, but not the solution below. This problem can be solved by improved engineering of the system, giving better flow and depth.

Root death can be solved by drying roots occasionally by turning off the pump, or by partial draining of the system so that only part of the roots are submerged, allowing more oxygen to the roots. The use of a warm solution would also provide more oxygen to the roots, since warm water holds more oxygen than a cold solution.

⊛   *The Hygro-Flo$^{(TM)}$ System.*[31] The principle of this system, like that of the NFT, confines the tomato root in a flexible black polyethylene tube through which the nutrient solution flows. The solution is circulated by a pump and gravity system. Nutrient solu-

31 Hygroponics, Inc., 3935 North Palo Alto Avenue, Panama City, Florida 32407.

Figure 79. *The Hygro-flo* ^(TM) *system. This is a modification of the nutrient film technique for hydroponic tomato production.* (HYDROPONICS, INC., 3935 N. PALO ALTO AVENUE, PANAMA CITY, FLORIDA 32407).

tions flow 24 hours a day—10 minutes on and 5 minutes off. The tubes are laid on wooden platforms sloped at 1 inch per 8 linear feet. Ends of the tube are allowed to hang into a polyvinyl chloride return gutter which is sloped so that the solution returns to the nutrient reservoir. The reservoir extends the length of the greenhouse and one end of the platform is laid above it (Fig. 79).

Plants are grown in cellulose growing blocks (BR–8 block) [32] 1 to 2 inches tall. These are placed in pre-cut slits of the tubing. The block holds up the plant and the nutrient circulates around the roots. "Dike sticks" are placed crosswise under the tubing to prevent the solution from bypassing the blocks during early plant growth stages. After 2–3 weeks, the sticks are removed and are placed over the tubing to help support the plants as the plants are lowered. The nutrient solution is delivered to the tubing under pressure from the main line through "spaghetti tubes."

Through the use of two proportioners placed in series, the nutrient concentrate is mixed at a rate of 2 gallons to 128 gallons of water into the reservoir. The solution is changed weekly. Between changes, the roots are washed by circulating water of pH 6.0 for

[32] Famco, Inc., Medina, Ohio.

24 hours. The nutrient solution and the pH level must be monitored each day, as prescribed.

OUTLOOK: REFLECTIONS AND PROJECTIONS

The potential for greenhouse tomato production has never been so great, nor problems more critical. The energy crisis, threats of high labor costs, large initial investments, excessive overhead and taxation, and competition from the outdoor and shipped in product continue at an accelerated pace.

Until recently, the competition for greenhouse tomatoes was primarily from Florida and Texas, where trellised and vine ripened fruit is harvested until mid-June. A new contender has now entered the ring. The volume of tomato imports from Mexico has increased fourfold (from 66 to 265 million pounds) in the last ten years; Mexican tomatoes now account for over twelve percent of the total U.S. production (2,056 million pounds) of tomatoes for the fresh market. Greenhouse-grown tomatoes contribute only five percent. Moreover, since these tomatoes come into the United States during the fall, winter and spring, they are in direct competition with greenhouse tomatoes. The value of tomato imports from Mexico now equals, or surpasses, that of the winter crop produced in Florida. Mexican tomatoes also compete with the spring crop produced in Florida, Texas, and California.

There are several reasons for the recent transition of the Mexican vegetable industry from subsistence production to a large supplier of winter tomatoes in the United States.

(1) New lands have been opened in the northwest states of Senora and Sinaloa where the lack of rain in winter, mild temperatures, adequate labor, abundant sunlight and water provide ideal growing conditions.

(2) Active research, demonstrations, and training programs have been sponsored by the Mexican Agricultural Institute and the Rockefeller Foundation.

(3)The increase in production costs in the United States has been accompanied by a dwindling labor supply.

(4) The impact of the cherry tomato, its production potential in Mexico, and an increasing demand in the United States have

hastened the growth of the Mexican industry. The cherry tomato can be harvested red and shipped without bruising, has high quality, is hardy, firm when ripe, prolific, and high yielding and may be the first type of tomato to be harvested mechanically for the fresh market.

It could have been, and probably was, predicted twenty years ago that the greenhouse tomato would become extinct as a result of increased production technology, rapid and controlled-atmosphere transport, improved varieties for outdoor production, and foreign imports. In fact, the price paid per pound of tomatoes did not change appreciably for twenty-five years (Fig. 59). The price remained, with minor fluctuations, at about twenty-five cents per pound, or two dollars for an eight-pound basket, as an average for all grades and sizes. This means, however, a price received per unit of scarcely half of that twenty-five years ago because of the decreased purchasing power of the dollar in goods and services. The only exceptions were in 1967, when returns averaged close to two dollars and twenty-five cents per basket, and 1968, when the returns approached the 1967 figure. Since 1970, prices have risen slowly, but lag far behind the precipitous increases in cost for heating and labor (Fig. 59).

What has enabled the greenhouse tomato industry to multiply its acreage during this period of steadily increasing costs? The answer lies in the remarkable increases in yield and quality. New varieties have been created with multiple disease resistance. Major breakthroughs have occurred in establishing optimal nutrient values and in maintaining them through soil and leaf tissue analyses and the application of all-soluble fertilizers through drip or trickle irrigation systems. Carbon dioxide enrichment at 1000–1200 ppm has become standardized. New plant growing techniques and culture media have been developed along with artificial mixes for improved root growth. Optimal temperature, light, and moisture requirements for flower formation and fruiting have been established. Effective biological control methods now exist for white fly and red spider mites. Significant achievements have occurred in greenhouse design and construction. Plastics (polyethylene and polyvinyl chloride films) and fiberglass were created. A new type of wide-paneled glass greenhouse (The Noordland)[33] has been introduced, and can be constructed at much less the cost of a standard glass structure.

[33] Medford, New York 11763.

A revolutionary development with far-reaching implications for greenhouse tomato culture has resulted from joint efforts by the University of Arizona, the University of Sonora (Mexico), and the Rockefeller Foundation. Located in the fishing community of Puerto Penasco on the Gulf of California, the project involved a unique combination of power, food, and water and production economics. Inflated double-unit plastic greenhouses (each half is twenty-five by one hundred feet) were built from twelve mil polyethylene attached to wood strips bolted onto a concrete footing (Fig. 80, 81). The estimated capital investment originally (1967) was only fifteen cents per square foot. The enclosed plants are grown in an atmospheric environment of approximately one hundred percent relative humidity and 1,000 ppm of carbon dioxide. This environment reduces the water requirement one to five percent of normal and greatly enhances growth rates and productivity. The Puerto Penasco project has the advantage of low construction costs, an unlimited amount of sea water for cooling in the summer and heating in the winter, the utilization of diesel fuel for the generation of electricity, and the desalination of sea water with carbon dioxide as a byproduct, along with the innovation of growing plants at one hundred percent relative humidity which reduces the normal fresh water requirement to a mere fraction. Given the possibility of year-round production under high intensity sunlight in a carbon dioxide enriched atmosphere almost every day of the year and the existence of eighteen thousand and five hundred miles of essentially uninhabited desert shoreline, the implications of this project are intriguing. This model, with some changes, has now been replicated in other desert areas (Fig. 82).

Vast improvements in greenhouse heating, ventilation, air circulation, the utilization of perforated plastic tubing, air conditioning, and automatic temperature controls have been adopted. Further improvements will undoubtedly occur.

New hybrid varieties resistant to Fusarium wilt, Verticillum wilt leaf mold (*Cladosporium fulvum*), and recently tobacco mosaic virus have been introduced. The most spectacular increases from any growth factor yet manipulated in the culture of greenhouse crops occurred in the early 1960's when carbon dioxide enrichment of greenhouse atmospheres began to be adopted. Carbon dioxide enrichment has been accompanied by new innovations in heating, ventilation, air circulation, and the control of moisture and nutrient

Figure 80. *Aerial view of the plastic greenhouse installations at Puerto Peñasco on the Gulf of California in Sonora, Mexico. Note the facility for desalination of sea water and the generation of electricity and carbon dioxide in the upper left corner.*

Figure 81. *Entrance to the inflated double unit 10 mil plastic greenhouses (25' x 100') at Puerto Peñasco. Capital investment for construction of these greenhouses was estimated at 15 cents per square foot in 1968.*

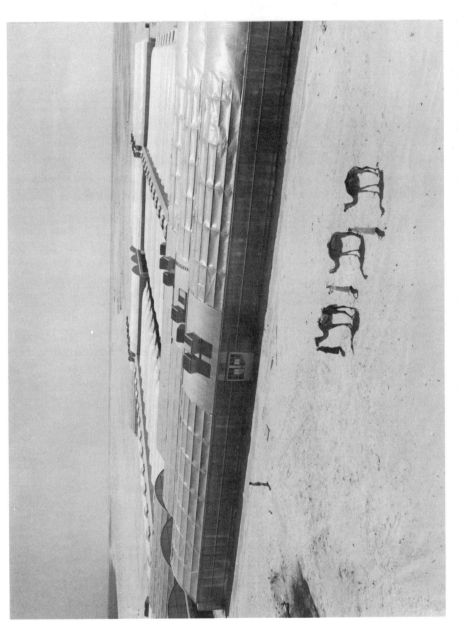

Figure 82. *The government of Abu Dhabi's 5-acre controlled environment greenhouse facility on Sadiyat Island, Abu Dhabi, United Arab Emirates.* (COURTESY ENVIRONMENTAL RESEARCH LABORATORY, UNIVERSITY OF ARIZONA, TUCSON, ARIZONA, U.S.A. *8576*).

levels. These developments and others have made it possible for the greenhouse tomato producer to double his yields and maintain a competitive position with the outdoor producer. The recent innovations in cultural media and biological controls for important insect pests have had a major impact on productivity in western Europe (Table 30).

The future will see a shift towards more automation in greenhouse tomato production. New hybrid varieties will be developed with multiple disease resistance and superior horticultural characteristics. The need for soil or root media sterilization may be eliminated. There will continue to be innovations in construction methods and the use of materials. Carbon dioxide additions, regulations, and controls will continue as important as those for temperature, mineral nutrients, and water. Research relating to a reduction of heat losses and energy conservation will take top priority. It is not too early to envision additional breakthroughs in mechanization of operations for greenhouse-grown tomatoes. Commercial acreages will continue to expand, chiefly in those areas with favorable freight rates, low land values, a potential labor supply, mild winter temperatures, little atmospheric pollution, high sunlight intensities during the fall, winter, and spring, and the capability for air conditioning through a naturally low atmospheric humidity. The dispersion of the industry noted during the past 10 years will continue. More refined cultural technologies will be adopted, including the use of rock wool, peat modules, and eventually the nutrient film technique—the most sophisticated of all hydroponic technologies. Markets will continue to grow, and year-round production of a high-quality product can become a reality.

LITERATURE ON THE CULTURE AND MARKETING OF GREENHOUSE-GROWN TOMATOES

Books, General References, and Proceedings of Conferences

Allerton, Frank W. *Tomato Growing.* 202 pp. Faber and Faber, Ltd. 24 Russell Square, London, England. 1959.

Anonymous. *Greenhouse Vegetable Production Recommendations.* Publication 365. Ontario Department of Agriculture and Food, Parliament Bldg., Toronto, Ontario, Canada. 1978.

Bewley, W. R. *Commercial Glasshouse Crops.* 509 pp. Country Life Limited, 2–10, Taristock St., Covent Garden, London, England. 1963.

Burt, A. C. *Modern Potting Composts.* George Allen and Unwin Ltd., London, 277 pp. 1976.

Dalrymple, Dana, G. *Controlled Environment Agriculture: A Global Review of Greenhouse Food Production.* Foreign Economic Report No. 89. USDA Foreign Development Division, Economic Research Service. Washington, D.C. 1973.

Dorey, R. *Tomato Growing by Prescription.* 167 pp. Blandford Press Limited. 16 West Central St., London, WC 1, England. 1960.

Flawn, L. W. *Tomato Ring Culture.* 78 pp. W. and G. Foley, Ltd. 110–125. Charing Cross Road, London WC 2, England. 1961.

Gaines, F. G., Jr. *Growing Greenhouse Tomatoes Commercially with Hydroponics.* Pan American Hydroponics, Inc. Grapevine, Texas. 1966.

Hallig, V. A. and C. Fich. *Tomato Under Glass.* 135 pp. Alm. Dansk Gartnerforenings Bogflorlag, Copenhagen, Denmark. 1961. (In Danish).

Hallig. V. A. and E. Jensen. *Tomatoes 1975.* University of Copenhagen, Denmark. 1976. 58 pp. (In Danish).

Hanan, J. J., W. D. Holley and K. L. Goldsberry. *Greenhouse Management.* 560 pp. Springer–Verlog, New York, 1978.

Hudson, J. P. (editor). *Control of the Plant Environment.* 240 pp. Academic Press, Inc., New York. 1957.

International Research and Technology Corporation. *An Assessment of Controlled Environment Agriculture Technology.* Submitted to the National Science Foundation under Contract No. C–1028, Feb. 17, 1978, Washington, D.C. Participants: L. H. deBivort, T. B. Taylor, and M. Fontes, 462 pp. 1978.

Horticultural Advisory Service. *Trough Culture.* Isle of Guernsey. St. Peter Port. 1971.

Jensen, Merle H. *Ring and Trough Culture for Greenhouse Tomato Production.*

Environmental Research Laboratory, The University of Arizona, Tucson, Arizona. 1968.

Jones, L. *Home Hydroponics and How to Do It.* 156 pp. Beardsley Publishing Co., Paradise Valley, Arizona. 1975.

Kingham, H. G. *The U.K. Tomato Manual.* 223 pp. Growers Books, 49 Doughty St., London WC 1 N 2P, England. 1973.

Lawrence. W. J. C. *Soil Sterilization.* 166 pp. MacMillan Co., 60 Fifth Ave., New York, N.Y. 1956.

Lindquist, R. K. and J. D. Farley. *Insect and Disease Control on Greenhouse Vegetables.* Ohio Cooperative Extension Service Bulletin 517. 1978.

McCullagh, J. C. (Editor). *The Solar Greenhouse Book.* 320 pp. Rodale Press, Emmaus, Pennsylvania. 1978.

Midwest Greenhouse Vegetable Conference Proceedings. Ohio Greenhouse Vegetable Growers Association, September 12–15, 1971.

Proceedings, First Northeast Greenhouse Vegetable Conference, Monmouth Junction, New Jersey, October 26–27. 1966. (Compiled by Merle H. Jensen).

Proceedings, Second Biennial Northeast Greenhouse Vegetable Conference, Windsor, Ontario, Canada, October 22–23, 1968. (Compiled by Ian D. W. Smith).

Proceedings, North American Greenhouse Vegetable Conference, Pittsburgh, Pennsylvania, September 28–October 1, 1970. (Compiled by Robert F. Fletcher).

Proceedings, Solar Energy—Fuel and Food Workshop, Environmental Research Laboratory, University of Arizona, Tucson, Arizona, April 5–6, 1976. 262 pp. (Merle H. Jensen, ed.).

Proceedings of a Conference on Solar Energy for Heating Greenhouses and Greenhouse-Residential Combinations. Cleveland and Wooster, Ohio. March 20–23, 1977. T. H. Short, *ed.* Ohio State University.

Proceedings of the International Symposium on Controlled-Environment Agriculture, Environmental Research Laboratory, University of Arizona, Tucson, Arizona, April 7–8, 1977. 413 pp. (Compiled by Merle H. Jensen).

Proceedings of the Southwest Greenhouse Vegetable Conference, Phoenix, Arizona – 1969; San Antonio, Texas – 1970; Las Vegas, Nevada – 1971.

Rees, A. R., K. E. Cockshull, D. W. Hand, R. G. Hurd. *Crop Processes in Controlled Environments.* Academic Press, N.Y. 391 pp. 1972.

Searle, S. A. *Plant, Climate and Irrigation.* 154 pp. Chichester Press Ltd. Chichester, England. 1954.

Symposium on Protected Growing of Vegetables. Plovdiv, Bulgaria. 402 pp. International Society for Horticultural Science, The Hague, Netherlands. May 5–10, 1969.

Swartz, M. *Guide to Commercial Hydroponics.* 136 pp. Israel Universities Press, N.Y. 1968.

Tennessee Valley Greenhouse Vegetable Workshop, Chattanooga, Tennessee, Tennessee Valley Authority, March 18–20, 1976.

Tiessen, H., Wiebe J., and C. Fisher. *Greenhouse Vegetable Production in Ontario.* Ontario Ministry of Agriculture and Food Publication 526. Toronto, Canada, 1976.

Walls, Ian G. *Tomato Growing Today.* 239 pp. David & Charles Limited. South Devon House, Newton Abbot, Devon, England. 1972.

Wittwer, S. H. and S. Honma. *Greenhouse Tomatoes—Guidlines for Successful Production.* Michigan State University Press, East Lansing, Michigan. 95 pp. 1969.

Bulletins, Circulars, Journal Articles, Research Reports:

Adams, P. and G. W. Winsor. Further Studies of the Composition and Quality of Tomato Fruit. Glasshouse Crops Research Institute Annual Report, pp. 133–138. 1976.

Alexander, L. J. and G. L. Oakes. New Tomato Varieties Resistant to TMV. Ohio Agr. Res. and Dev. Ctr., Ohio, Report 55:32–35. 1970.

Alexander, L. J. and J. D. Farley. Ohio M–R 13: A New Greenhouse Tomato Variety Resistant to Five Ohio Strains of TMV. Ohio Agr. Res. and Dev. Ctr. Res. Bul. 1057. 1972.

Anonymous. Insect Control on Greenhouse Vegetables. Ohio Agr. Res. and Dev. Ctr. Bul. 517. 1974.

Bandadyga and C. H. Miller. Growing Tomatoes in Plastic Greenhouses. North Carolina State Agr. Ext. Serv. Cir. 1974.

Barmettler, E. R., G. D. Robison, F. W. Bunker, R. Post and C. Mills. A Budgetary Analysis of Agricultural Production Under Controlled Environmental Conditions. Univ. of Nevada (Reno) Special Report 1969.

Bauerle, W. L., and T. H. Short. Conserving Heat in Glass Greenhouses with Surface-Mounted Air-Inflated Plastic. Ohio Agricultural Research and Development Center. Special Circular 101. 1977.

Beddal, D. J. Tomatoes on Peat Mattress. Kent Agricultural Development and Adv. Serv. Tech. Info. 75/4. 1975 (England).

Blassingame, Donald. Disease of Greenhouse Tomatoes and Their Control. Mississippi State Univ. Agr. Ext. Service. 1973.

Blassingame, Donald. Principles of Soil Fumigation in the Greenhouse. Mississippi State Univ. Agr. Ext. Service. 1973.

Brooks, W. M. Growing Greenhouse Tomatoes in Ohio. Ohio State University Coop. Ext. Serv. Pub. SB–19. 1973.

Burns, E. R., R. S. Pile, Carl E. Madewell, J. B. Martin, and Johnny Carter. Using Power Plant Discharge Water in Controlled Environment Greenhouses. Progress Report II. Tennessee Valley Authority, Muscle Shoals, Alabama. 1976.

Cooper, A. J. Rapid Progress Through 1974 with Nutrient Film Trials. Grower 83:186–188. 1975.

Cooper, A. J. Nutrient Film Technique of Growing Crops. Grower Books, London, 33 pp. 1976.

Cooper, A. J. and R. R. Charlesworth. Nutritional Control of a Nutrient Film Tomato Crop. Scientia Horticulturae 7:189–195. 1977.

Corgan, J. N., F. B. Widomoyer and G. M. Burke. Greenhouse Tomatoes. New Mexico State Univ. Coop. Ext. Ser. Cir. 387. 1967.

Cotter, J. and R. T. Seay. The Effect of Circulating Air on the Environment and Tomato Growth Response in a Plastic Greenhouse. Proc. Amer. Soc. Hort. Sci. 77:643–646. 1961.

Cravens, M. E. Comparison of Economics of Winter Production of Horticultural Products in Greenhouses in the USA with Outdoor Production in Areas Distant from the Market. Outlook on Agr. 8:39–94. 1974.

Courter, J. W., J. S. Vandemark and R. A. Hinton. The Feasibility of Growing Greenhouse Tomatoes in Southern Illinois. Univ. of Ill. Coop. Ext. Cir. 914. 1965.

Dedolph, R. R. and H. E. Larzelere. Tomatoes—Color Development and Consumer Preference. Michigan Agr. Exp. Sta. Quart. Bul. 45:219–222. 1961.

Dhillon, P. S. and P. J. Kirschling. Profitability of Tomato Production Under Plastic Greenhouses. Cook College, Rutgers Univ. A.E. 335. 1971.

Dhillon, P. S. Cost of Producing Tomatoes in Plastic Greenhouses in New Jersey. Cook College, Rutgers University A.E. 328. 1970.

Ellis, N. K., Merle Jensen, John Larsen and Norman F. Oebker. Nutriculture Systems. Purdue University Agricultural Experiment Station Bulletin No. 44. West Lafayette, Indiana, 1974.

Fisher, G. A. Greenhouse Vegetable Production in Ontario. Production Costs and Returns to Risk and Management. Ontario Ministry of Agriculture and Food, Toronto. 1975.

Glasshouse Crops Research Institute. The Biological Control of Tomato Pests. Growers Bulletin No. 3. Littlehampton, Sussex, England. 1976.

Hartman, J. R. and A. S. Williams. Guide for Chemical Control of Vegetable Diseases. Univ. of Kentucky Pub. 1975.

Harssema, H. Root Temperatures and Growth of Young Tomato Plants. Meded. Landbou. Wageningen 17–19 (1977). 85 pp.

Honma, S., H. H. Murakishi and S. H. Wittwer. Moto-Red—A Tobacco Mosaic Virus Resistant Greenhouse Tomato. Mich. Agr. Exp. Sta. Quart. Bul. 50:285–287. 1968.

Honma, S. and H. H. Murakishi. Rapids—Greenhouse Tomato Resistant to TMV. Mich. Agr. Exp. Sta. Res. Rpt. 126. 1971.

Honma, S., J. D. Vriesenga and R. C. Herner. High Density Tomato Production. Amer. Veg. Grower 20(3):34, 36. 1972.

Jacobs, J. M. and D. Meyaard. Economical Aspects of Protected Cultivation. Acta Horticulturae 51:349–361. 1975.

Jensen, M. H. The Use of Polyethylene Barriers Between Soil and Growing Medium in Greenhouse Vegetable Production. Univ. of Arizona. 1971.

Jensen, M. H. Energy Alternatives and Conservation for Greenhouses. Hort-Science 12(1):14–23. 1977.

Jensma, J. R. Methods of Glasshouse Production in Holland. Bruinsma Bulletin, Naaldwijk. 1958.

Johnson, H., Jr. Greenhouse Vegetable Production. Univ. of Calif. Agr. Ext. Service. OSA 249. 1972.

Kerr, E. A. and J. K. Muehmer. Veegan Hybrid Greenhouse Tomato Report of the Horticultural Exp. Sta. and Products. Lab. Vineland Station, Ontario. 1964.

Lambeth, V. N. Breeding Quality Tomatoes for Greenhouse Forcing. VeeGee Messenger, February, 1962. pp. 2, 9. 1962.

Lambeth, V. N. Tuckcross 520. Missouri Agr. Exp. Sta. Spec. Rept. 86. 1967.

Larsen, J. E., C. D. Welch and C. Gray. A New Approach to Fertilizing Greenhouse Tomatoes. Texas Agr. Ext. Service Inf. Reprt. 16. 1968.

Larsen, J. E. Growing Tomatoes in Plastic Greenhouses. Texas Agr. Ext. Service. 1970.

Larsen, J. E. A Peat-Vermiculite Mix for Growing Transplants and Vegetables in Trough Culture. Texas Agr. Ext. Serv. 1971.

Larzelere, H. E. and R. R. Dedolph. Consumers Acceptance of Greenhouse Grown and Southern Field-Grown Tomatoes. Mich. Agr. Exp. Sta. Quart. Bul. 44:554–558. 1962.

Liner, H. H. and A. A. Bandyga. Costs and Returns from Producing Greenhouse Tomatoes in North Carolina. North Carolina Agr. Ext. Serv. 1974.

Lucas, R. E. and S. H. Wittwer. Soil and Plant Tissue Nutrient Levels as Indices of Fertilizer Requirement for the Production of Greenhouse Tomatoes. Mich. Agr. Exp. Sta. Quart. Bul. 45:595–607. 1963.

Lucas, R. E., S. H. Wittwer and F. G. Teubner. Maintaining High Soil Nutrient Levels for Greenhouse Tomatoes Without Excess Salt Accumulation. Soil Sci. Soc. Amer. Proc. 25:214–218. 1960.

Lucas, R. E., P. E. Rieke and E. C. Doll. Soil Saturated Extract Method for Determining Plant-Nutrient Levels in Peat and Other Mixes. Proc. 4th Int'l. Peat Congr. 3:221–230. 1972.

Maas, E. F., and R. M. Adamson. Soilless Culture of Commercial Greenhouse Tomatoes. Canada Dept. of Agr. Pub. 1460. 1971.

Maes, R. E. A large scale northern climate solar garden. Environmental Research Institute of Michigan, Ann Arbor 48107. 1977.

McElroy, R. G., J. E. Pallas, Jr. and W. K. Trotter. Economics of Greenhouse

Tomato Production in the Southeast. Economics, Statistics, and Cooperative Service, U.S. Department of Agriculture ESCS–02. 1978.

Moore, E. L. Obtaining Fruit Set of Plastic Greenhouse Tomatoes. Miss. Agr. Exp. Sta. Bul. 768. 1968.

Moore, E. L. Tomato Varieties Suited for Greenhouse Forcing. Miss. Agr. Exp. Sta. Inf. Sheet 1185. 1972.

Morgan, J. V. and E. J. Clarke. Influence of Stage of Development on Flowering and Fruiting in Tomato. Acta Horticulturae 51:131–149. 1975.

Muehmer, J. K. and E. A. Kerr. Vendor, A. Greenhouse Tomato Resistant to Tobacco Mosaic Virus in Ontario. Ann. Rept. Hort. Res. Inst. Ontario, pp. 52–54. 1967.

Murakishi, H. H. Comparative Incidence of Graywall and Internal Browning of Tomato and Sources of Resistance. Phytopathology 50:408–412. 1960.

New, L. and R. E. Roberts. Automatic Drip Irrigation for Greenhouse Tomato Production. Texas Agr. Exp. Sta. Bul. MP 1082. 1973.

Norton, J. D. Effect of Soil Temperature on Greenhouse Tomato Production. Alabama Agr. Exp. Sta. Highlights of Agricultural Research 17:2. 1970.

O'Dell, C. R. Soilless Culture of Greenhouse Tomatoes. Virginia Polytechnic Institute Ext. Div. Pub. MH.

Peck, J. F., M. R. Fontes, N. G. Hicks and M. Hopkins. A New Continuous-string Method of Plant Tying in Greenhouses. HortScience 8:471–472. 1973.

Partyka, R. E. and L. J. Alexander. Ohio State Coop. Ext. Ser. SB 16. 1972.

Phatak, S. C., S. H. Wittwer and F. C. Teubner. Top and Root Temperature Effects on Tomato Flowering. Proc. Amer. Soc. Hort. Sci. 88:527–531. 1966.

Roll-Hansen, J. Fritted Trace Elements (FTE) as a Basic Fertilizer for Peat. Paper presented at the I.S.H.S. Symposium Peat in Horticulture, Noordwijk, The Netherlands. 1975.

Rudd-Jones, D. Root Environment Control: Nutrient Film Culture. Proceedings of the International Symposium on Controlled Environment Agriculture, pp. 216–224. University of Arizona, Tucson, Arizona, April 7–8, 1977.

Sangster, D. M. Soilless Culture of Tomatoes with Slow-release Fertilizers. Ontario Min. of Agr. and Food. Factsheet Agdex 291/518. 1973.

Schales, F. D. and P. H. Massey, Jr. Tomato Production in Plastic Greenhouses. Virginia Polytechnic Institute Ext. Div. Pub. 154. 1968.

Sheldrake, R., Jr. and S. Dallyn. Production of Greenhouse Tomatoes in Ring and Trough Cultures. Cornell Veg. Crops Mimeo No. 149. 1969.

Sheldrake, R., Jr., S. L. Dallyn and D. Sangster. Slow-release Fertilizer for Greenhouse Tomatoes. New York's Food and Life Sciences 4(2, 3):10. 1971.

Smith, P. M. Greenhouse Tomato Production. Alabama Agr. Exp. Sta. Ext. Cir. P–95.

Spivey, C. D., J. B. Jones, J. M. Barber and Paul Colditz. Growing Tomatoes in a Protective Structure. Georgia Agr. Exp. Sta. Coop. Ext. Leaflet 184. 1974.

Stadhonders, P. J. Priorities in Research for Protected Cultivation. Chronica Horticulturae 16(1/2):1–2. 1976.

Stoner, A. K. Commercial Production of Greenhouse Tomatoes. USDA. Agr. Handbook 382. 1971.

Sullivan, G. H. and J. L. Robertson. Production, Marketing, and Economic Trends in the Tomato Industry. Purdue University Agr. Exp. Sta. Res. Bul. 908. 1974.

Taylor, G. A. and R. L. Flannery. Growing Greenhouse Tomatoes in a Peat-Vermiculite Media. Cook College, Rutgers Univ. Veg. Crop Offset Series 33. Rev. 1970.

University of California. Greenhouse Tomato Production Leaflet 2806. Berkeley, California. 1975.

Van Heyningen Bros. Ltd. Assessment of Trading Result Year Ended 31st. October 1976. Littlehampton, Sussex, England. 1977.

Verwer, F. L. J. A. W. Growing Vegetable Crops in Rock Wool and Other Media. Acta Horticulturae 50:61–67. 1975.

Vincent, C. L. Growing Tomatoes in Greenhouses. Wash. Agr. Exp. Sta. Cir. 276. 1961.

Ward, G. M. Fertilizer Schedule for Greenhouse Tomatoes in Southwestern Ontario. Canada Dept. Agri. Publ. No. 1237. 1965.

Welch, N. C. Growing Tomatoes in Plastic Greenhouse. Univ. Calif. Ext. Ser. Bernadino Co. 1965.

Wiebe, John. Greenhouse Vegetable Production on Ontario. Ontario Department of Agriculture and Food Publication 526. 1971.

Wittwer, S. H. Carbon Dioxide and its Role in Plant Growth. Proc. XVII Int'l. Hort. Cong. Vol. III, 311–322. 1967.

Wittwer, S. H. Photoperiod and Flowering in the Tomato (*Lycopersicon esculentum*). Proc. Amer. Soc. Hort. Sci. 83:688–694. 1963.

Wittwer, S. H. Practices for Increasing the Yields of Greenhouse Tomatoes. Mich. Agr. Exp. Sta. Cir. 228. 1960.

Wittwer, S. H. Tomato Production in Plastic Greenhouses—Opportunity with Problems. Proc. 1963 Agr. Plastics Conf. 1963.

Wittwer, S. H. and L. G. Aung. Flowering of Tomato. From: Induction of Flowering—Case Histories. L. G. Evans, Editor. 1969.

Wittwer, S. H. and W. R. Robb, Carbon Dioxide Enrichment of Greenhouse Atmospheres for Food Crop Production. Econ. Bot. 18:34–56. 1964.

Wittwer, S. H. and F. G. Teubner. Cold Exposure of Tomato Seedlings and Flower Formation. Proc. Amer. Soc. Hort. Sci. 67:369–376. 1956.

Wittwer, S. H. Carbon dioxide fertilization of crop plants. *In*: Crop Physiology.

U. S. Gupta, Ed., pp. 310–333. Oxford and IBH Publishing Co., 66 Janpath, New Delhi, India. 1977.

Annual Reports, Yearbooks, Communications, and Special Editions of Magazines

American Vegetable Grower, November issues, Willoughby, Ohio 44049.
Environmental Research Laboratory, University of Arizona, Tucson.
Glasshouse Crops Research Institute, Rustington, Littlehampton, Sussex, England.
Grower, 49 Doughty St., London WCIN 2LP, England.
Guernsey Growers Association. Cambridge Bert. White Rak Guernsey.
John Innes Horticultural Institute, Hertford, Herts, England.
Naaldwijk Glasshouse Crops Experiment Station. Naaldwijk, Holland.
Ohio Agricultural Research and Development Center, Greenhouse Vegetable Field Day, Research Summaries. Wooster, Ohio 44691.
Stockbridge House Experimental Horticulture Station. Cawood, Selby, North Yorkshire, England.
Outlook in Agriculture 8(2)54–116. Imperial Chemical Industries—Plant Protection Limited, Jealott's Hill Research Station. 1974.

More Recent References

American Vegetable Grower and Greenhouse Grower. Richard T. Meister, Ed. Is Hydroponics the Answer? 26(11):11–16. 1978.
Brooks, C. The Nutrient Film Technique. 1978 Annual Report and Year Book Guernsey Growers Association, pp. 44–52. St. Peter Port, Guernsey. 1978.
Protected Cultivation in Japan. Y. Mihara, Ed. International Symposium on Potential Productivity in Protected Cultivation, 36 pp. Kyoto and Tokyo, August, 1978.
Schippers, P. A. Soilless Growing in Europe. American Vegetable Grower and Greenhouse Grower 26(12):17–18. 1978.
Spensley, K., G. W. Winsor and A. J. Cooper. Nutrient Film Technique—Crop Culture in Flowing Nutrient Solution. Outlook on Agriculture 9(6): 299–305. 1978.
Widmer, R. E. Warm Water Greenhouse Heating. American Vegetable Grower and Greenhouse Grower 26(11):34, 62. 1978.

❧ GREENHOUSE LETTUCE

Greenhouse lettuce is one of the oldest and more important vegetable crops. It is adapted for growing during the coldest and darkest months of the year. For the northern hemisphere, this is from September to April. Prior to the use of polyethylene, fiberglass, and polyvinyl chloride houses, lettuce was grown under glass. With the influx of non-glass houses, the industry took a sudden growth mainly because of the low cost in putting up the protected structure.

Greenhouse lettuce is almost universally grown in rotation or as a companion crop (Fig. 83) with tomatoes, or in rotation with bedding plants. Occasionally, growers specialize only in greenhouse lettuce production. In Europe, there are those who specialize in the growing of greenhouse lettuce the year-round.

The production of high quality greenhouse lettuce is an exact and expensive venture. Both practical and technical knowledge is required. It can be a profitable business for the progressive grower.

❧ PROTECTED STRUCTURES

Glasshouses provide an environment in which lettuce can be grown all year. However, with the influx of plastics, many types of polyethylene, polyvinyl chloride, and fiberglass houses are being used (Fig. 63). These structures have a lower initial investment. In the case of polyethylene, there is an annual cost of covering and repairing the structure. Polyvinyl chloride and fiberglass covering, however, have a longer life. Since lettuce is grown during the cooler cloudy months of the year, proper choice of material should be used

Figure 83. *Greenhouse lettuce is often grown as a companion crop to tomatoes. In this photograph Grand Rapids and Bibb lettuce is alternatively planted between rows of tomatoes.*

Figure 84. *Year-round greenhouse lettuce production in Denmark. Photographed July 1977.*

Figure 85. *Two strains of Grand Rapids type greenhouse lettuce. Left, H-54 tip burn resistant; right, Waldmann's Green.* (RICHARD PRETZER GREENHOUSES, CLEVELAND, OHIO, MARCH *1978*).

to supply maximum transmission of light. Alternatives in structures, ventilation, air circulation, and heating should be considered.

A sandy loam soil high in organic matter is preferable for lettuce production. A drainage system is essential and can be had by installing 4 inch clay tile 14 inches deep and 18 inches apart with a slope of one inch per 100 feet. The same tiles can be used for steam sterilization if provided with a steam header at the time of installation. Plastic tiles can be used for drainage. They are not recommended for soil sterilization.

To maintain a loose friable soil, organic matter—such as rotted manure, chopped hay, or peanut hulls—must be added once a year. The structures should be so constructed that the ground beds can be fertilized and tilled with large equipment prior to sterilization.

෮ VARIETIES

Both leaf and butterhead types are used for greenhouse forcing. They are adapted for production in plastic and glasshouses in North America. Although Cos types are not grown extensively, they could be with slight modifications of cultural practices.

⊛   *Leaf Lettuce.* The variety, Grand Rapids, had its origin from the variety Black Seeded Simpson. The selection was made by Eugene Davis in 1890 of Grand Rapids, Michigan. It remains today as the most famous and important of all greenhouse grown leaf lettuce varieties in North America. The variety was further selected by the late Rynard Yonker of Grand Rapids, Michigan, from which the Washington strain was developed.

This variety is widely adapted for growing in both plastic and glasshouses. Use of tip burn resistant strains has become popular in recent years. The latest selection, Grand Rapids H–54, is a tip burn resistant strain released by the Ohio Agricultural Experiment Station.

Waldmann's Green (Fig. 85) is a darker green and faster growing strain of Grand Rapids. It was selected by Mr. Waldmann of Cincinnati, Ohio. This variety is popular in the Indianapolis, Indiana, and in the Cincinnati and Cleveland, Ohio, areas; and in the northeastern U.S.A., but not in Michigan.

Tendergreen, a selection from a cross of Bibb and Grand Rapids, was introduced by the Michigan Agricultural Experiment Station in 1955. This variety is an intermediate between the leaf and the butterhead. This variety has not found general acceptance in the greenhouse industry, except for limited planting in the Minneapolis-St. Paul, Minnesota, area.

Domineer (Fig. 86) was introduced in 1972 by the Michigan Agricultural Experiment Station. This variety is a week to 10 days earlier than Grand Rapids H–54, and is tolerant to legginess at high temperatures and is more vigorous. The variety is a result of hybridizing Grand Rapids H–54 and the English variety, Chestnut 5B (Fig. 87), which is early and does well under low light conditions. The leaves of Domineer are slightly darker green than Grand Rapids, but lighter than Waldmann's Green. There is less frill on the leaf edge than with Grand Rapids. Since this variety is early and vigorous, it requires more water during the growing period than Grand Rapids. The variety has had only limited acceptance by the greenhouse industry, with small plantings in Michigan and larger plantings in Ontario, Canada.

⊛   *Butterhead.* In the Boston area, soft head types, commonly called butterhead, have been grown. Most of the industry has now disappeared. The varieties are similar to those used in Europe. The more popular varieties are Big Boston and May King. Another

Figure 86. *Domineer leaf lettuce for greenhouse production.*

Figure 87. *Greenhouse lettuce types. Left to right; Grand Rapids, Cheshunt 5-B, and Bibb.*

variety developed in Canada and grown in North America is Butter King, which is resistant to high temperature and bolting. Several European varieties such as Deci-minor and Ostinata have been successfully grown. Ostinata has also been successfully grown under completely controlled environments (Fig. 88).

Bibb is also a butterhead type and, since World War II, has be-

come increasingly popular. This variety was developed and introduced by Major John (Jack) Bibb in 1870. It was grown in his garden
in Frankfort, Kentucky, until his death in 1884 at the age of 95. A
group of growers in Frankfort maintained the strain until it was
accepted and listed by seed companies. Commercial Bibb production
originated near Louisville, Kentucky. In Michigan, the variety was
introduced in the 1940's by Maurice Chadwick of Grand Rapids. It
is said that he created a demand by distributing free samples to
hotels and restaurants. The J. W. Davis Company greenhouses in
Terre Haute, Indiana, began growing Bibb lettuce in 1951. They
were the nation's largest producers until the greenhouses were sold
in 1975. This variety is presently grown in greenhouses in Ohio,
Michigan, Indiana, and Kentucky.

There are many strains of Bibb lettuce now featured by seed
companies (Fig. 89). Some growers have their own selections. All
strains, however, show a close resemblance. The head is small, loosely
formed, and cup shaped. The outer leaves are dark green, thick, and
tender, often tinged with red when grown at cooler temperatures.
The variety is distinct in its color, buttery flavor, and crispness. All

Figure 88. *Butterhead (Ostinata) and Bibb lettuce grown to maturity under
completely controlled environments.* (RICHARD PRETZER, CLEVELAND, OHIO).

these characteristics vary from the outer leaves to the heart.

Buttercrunch and Summer Bibb are varieties closely related to Bibb. They have not, however, been satisfactory as forcing varieties in Michigan.

Chesibb (Fig. 90) was developed and introduced by the Michigan Agricultural Experiment Station in 1969. Cheshunt 5–B, an English variety with desirable head characteristics, and tolerance to low light intensity, was hybridized with Bibb. Plants were selected for earliness, vigor, head type, and less shattering and bruising leaf characteristics. This variety is less green and crisp than Bibb. The flavor is equal to Bibb, but it matures two weeks earlier.

❧ PLANTING SCHEDULES

Cropping systems tend to vary with the type of rotation the grower desires. Different areas in North America begin their tomato, cucumber, or bedding plants at various times of the year. The

Figure 89. *Strains of Bibb type lettuce. Left to right; Summer Bibb, Bibb, and Buttercrunch.*

schedules listed below and condensed in Table 37 show approximate times of transplanting and harvesting of lettuce. This table should be used as a guide in setting up the cropping schedule. Seeding dates have been omitted. However, approximately 30 to 45 days must be allowed between seeding and transplanting, depending on the season of the year.

Figure 90. *Chesibb lettuce for greenhouse production.*

Planting schedules vary from a single crop of lettuce in the fall to continuous cropping. Listed below are 5 different programs. They are summarized in Table 37.

I. A single fall crop of lettuce. Plants are set at the 3 to 4 leaf stage in late September. Harvest is late October or early November. After crop is removed, tomato plants can be set for an early spring crop. Many growers in the Cleveland and Toledo, Ohio, areas and in Essex County, Ontario, Canada, have adopted this schedule. High temperatures (above 85°F) in late summer often results in poor seed germination for this crop. Germination in warm soil can often be improved by placing moistened seed in a refrigerator at 40°F for 3 to 5 days prior to seeding.

More recently a practical way of preventing high temperature seed dormancy has been reported. Seeds are soaked for 15 minutes in a 70 to 100 ppm solution of kinetin and then dried. This will allow the seeds to germinate at high temperatures for up to one year. The treatment does not wet the seeds appreciably, but permits sufficient kinetin to be absorbed. The kinetin should be dissolved in a small quantity of ethyl alcohol prior to mixing it with water.

II. One mid-winter crop of lettuce. Where two crops of to-

TABLE 37. Planting schedules for greenhouse lettuce.

Schedule	Transplanting data	Crop harvest
I Lettuce	Sept. 15–30	Nov. 1–15
Early tomatoes	Nov. 15–30	Mar. 1
II Tomato	Aug. 25	Oct. 10–15
Lettuce	Jan. 1–15	Mar. 1–15
Tomato	Mar. 1–15	May 15–30
III Lettuce Bibb	Sept. 15–30	Oct. 15–30
Lettuce Leaf	Sept. 15–30	Nov. 1–15
Lettuce Bibb	Oct. 15–30	Dec. 15–30
Lettuce Leaf	Nov. 15–30	Feb. 15–28
Lettuce Bibb	Jan. 1–15	Feb. 15–28
Tomato	Mar. 1–15	May 15–30

IV Similar to III, except intercropping with tomato following the last harvest. Crops harvested late April to mid-May.

V Continuous lettuce crop

matoes are grown in a year, lettuce is planted in the ground bed following sterilization in mid-January and is harvested in early March. This schedule is being used by some growers in the Grand Rapids, Michigan, area.

III. Two full crops of Grand Rapids or three crops of Bibb. Such cropping schedules normally precede a mid to late spring tomato crop. The fall planting is grown as described in I above. This is followed by a second crop which is set in the ground bed in November and harvested in February. Three crops of Bibb which mature more rapidly than Grand Rapids may be grown by extending the time slightly. When this schedule is followed, a continuous harvest flow from late October to March is possible. The seed is sown every other day in August and early September and weekly thereafter till mid-October. With the advent of early maturing leaf lettuce types such as Domineer, and early maturing Bibb types such as Chesibb, the number of crops may be increased.

IV. Cropping schedule is similar to III above, but with an additional crop planted as an intercrop with tomatoes. Growers normally call it a half crop, since it is grown together with tomatoes. During February and to mid-March, the plants are set into rows in the ground bed followed by tomato plants a month later. After several weeks of companion crop growing, the lecture is harvested in April and early May. This plan is still used by many Michigan, Ohio, and Indiana growers.

V. Continuous cropping. This schedule is merely an extension of IV above. Some of the larger growers with adequate acreage harvest continuously from October to May or mid-June.

PLANT GROWING

Seedlings are grown in ground beds or on raised benches. If benches are used, a sandy loam with high organic matter is preferred. The soil should be friable so that, at the time of lifting, the separation of the transplants can be done with minimum injury to the roots. The seed bed should be sterilized prior to seeding. Lettuce seed is distributed evenly over the bed and covered with 1/4 inch of soil. Many growers sprinkle vermiculite or use cheese cloth. The cloth is kept damp and is removed when the seeds begin to germinate. Temperatures best suited for germination are 60–68°F. Where fresh lettuce seed is used, it is important to germinate in light.

Two plant growing procedures used depend on the season of the year. For the fall crop, seeds are sown thinly in open beds in the greenhouse or outside and the seedlings after 3 to 4 weeks are transplanted directly to the ground bed. Outside beds are normally used if an early fall crop is desired or the house cannot be directly used following soil sterilization. Where chemical fumigants are used to sterilize the ground beds, the houses are closed for one or two weeks. The disadvantage of using outdoor grown plants is that they may be infected with virus (aster yellows) if the plants are not kept sprayed to control the leafhoppers and aphids. The disease may not be visible at the time of transplanting, but becomes apparent several weeks after transplanting.

Bibb is often transplanted directly from the seed bed to the ground bed even in the winter (Fig. 91). Seedlings of uniform size should be transplanted, since the crop is harvested at one time for each planting.

Figure 91. *Bibb lettuce plants ready for transplanting into the ground beds.*

"Double rooting" or transplanting twice is a common practice during the winter months. Transplanting is expensive; however, it produces better plants. Seed is sown in small beds on raised benches. About a week after emergence, the seedlings are spaced 1 x 2 inches apart on benches or in beds, and are allowed to grow for 3 to 4 weeks. Double rooting economizes on greenhouse space, encourages selection of uniform plants, and permits the young plants to be grown at a slightly higher temperature in an area separated from the main growing area. Bibb lettuce plants should be grown at a night temperature of 60°F, while Grand Rapids should be maintained at about 55°F. Since the fuel oil and natural gas shortage and escalating energy costs, plants are being grown at 55 and 50° respectively. Lowering of the temperature delays the maturity of the crop.

The number of plants grown per acre depends on the spacing in the greenhouse beds (Table 38). In general, many more Bibb plants are needed than Grand Rapids at a given time of the year. The wider spacings are used in early fall and spring. Closer spacings are used in mid-winter. In winter, the heads of lettuce plants, especially Bibb, are small, hence the closer spacing. Recently, however, buyers insist on 28 to 30 heads of Bibb lettuce in a 5 pound box, which is normally attained with 6 x 6 inch spacing. Heads larger than these are discouraged. Plantings 6 x 6 and 7 x 7 inches are being used for Bibb, and 7 x 7 to 9 x 9 inches are generally used for leaf. Some growers plant closer in one direction than in the other to facilitate cultivation; however, planting on the square allows the plant to develop more uniformly.

Prior to setting the plants, the bed is moistened, fertilized, and tilled. A rake-like marker made with wooden pegs spaced at the proper distance is used. The rake is pulled parallel and perpendicular to the length of the greenhouse range (Fig. 92). Other types of markers such as pegs or narrow cross pieces of wood are also used. The use of a broad board with markers does not require boards for kneeling while the workers are transplanting.

The transplants are placed into the ground bed with the forefinger where the line crosses, or in holes made by the peg. The board is used to kneel on. As the area in front of the board is planted, the board is moved. The plants should not be set below the crown. Watering should be with a fine spray so as not to cover the leaves with soil.

Figure 92. *Marking rows (top) and planting (bottom) of lettuce.*

◉ *Soil-Block Technique.* A pelleted seed-soil-block system (Figs. 93, 94) for growing seedlings makes it possible to raise uniform lettuce plants in the shortest possible time. It is being used by many European growers. In the larger establishments, separate houses are used. For smaller growers, soil-block grown seedlings can be purchased from specialized plant growers.

Figure 93. *A soil block machine to produce blocks for seedling production* (DENMARK, *1977*).

Soil-blocks, with pelleted seed, are removed from a soil-block machine by use of a special lifting fork with a push bar attachment, and are laid on the floor of the greenhouse. Since the pellet seeding attachment is not perfect, a few seeds are missed and, therefore, it is necessary to drop a pellet in the missing blocks so that all of the blocks will have a pelleted seed. Pelleted seeds are three times as expensive as ordinary seed. It is, therefore, essential to obtain a high germinating seed lot. The advantage of using pelletized seed is the labor saved in thinning and seeding.

The blocks are covered with paper during the cooler months and

Figure 94. *Lettuce seedlings in soil blocks* (DENMARK, *1977*).

with a rigid sheet of polystyrene in the summer months to keep them cool. After the seeds germinate in about 3 days, the covering is removed. The germination temperature should be near 70°F.

The soil-block plants are planted in beds by hand or by use of a machine. With hand planting, a marker consisting of metal circles with short square block sections welded to the circle leaves a depression in the soil in which the soil-blocks are placed (Fig. 95). Several types of machines which carry one or more people mark the bed with square holes. These are being used in larger establishments. Those riding the machine drop the blocks into the holes. Three-fourths of the height of the block should be buried in sandy soils. For other types of soils, the depth of placing the soil-blocks is not

TABLE 38. Common spacings and number of lettuce plants per acre.

Distance between plants in inches	Approximate number of plants required per acre
Common spacings for Bibb	
6 × 6	175,000
6 × 7	150,000
6 × 8	130,000
7 × 7	130,000
7 × 8	112,000
Common spacings for Grand Rapids	
8 × 8	100,000
8 × 9	90,000
9 × 9	80,000

important as long as the block and the surface border soil are kept moist.

If the soil-block is made of 100 percent peat, it is important to keep the block moist, since once the block dries out, it is difficult to

Figure 95. *Soil-block grown lettuce spaced in the greenhouse* (DENMARK, *1977*).

re-wet. After the blocks are placed in beds, the blocks are kept moist by use of a fine spray of water from an overhead irrigation system. In a few days, the roots will emerge from the blocks and root into the soil.

❧ CULTURAL REQUIREMENTS

◎ *Soil Fertility and Lime.* One lettuce crop removes less nutrients from the soil than a greenhouse tomato crop. The high level of fertility recommended for greenhouse tomatoes has given good yields of lettuce, since lettuce is shallow rooted and grows rapidly. One heavy crop of lettuce removes approximately 60 to 80 pounds of actual nitrogen, 25 pounds of phosphorus, and 70 to 80 pounds of potassium per acre.

Rotted animal manure is recommended, if the soil does not have excess salts. Most growers add 50 to 100 yards of manure per acre in the fall when available and prior to soil sterilization. One should add to the soil approximately 40 pounds of actual nitrogen, 120 pounds of phosphorus, and 50 pounds of potassium before tilling. The proper amount should be determined from soil tests. For growers who use chemicals for soil sterilization, organic matter such as peat, peanut hulls, chopped hay are suggested. If the organic matter is not well decomposed, 10 to 15 of nitrogen should be added to facilitate decomposition.

Although a leafy crop such as lettuce uses large amounts of nitrogen, overfeeding will cause rank succulent growth and, in case of Bibb, the plant will develop as a Cos type without head formation. Succulent growth also makes the plant more subject to diseases.

Lettuce is sensitive to excess salts, but has a high calcium requirement. The crop is sensitive to a low pH or acid soil. If the pH is below 6.5, lime should be added to bring the range from 6.5 to 7.0. Lime may be applied as hydrated lime, ground burned limestone, or ground limestone. Ground burned limestone gives quick results, while ground limestone gives the slowest.

◎ *Watering.* Lettuce is shallow rooted and has a fiberous root system. It is essential that the crop receives adequate moisture. Thorough irrigation is recommended, rather than frequent light

Figure 96. Sclerotina *bottom rot ("drop") in Bibb and Grand Rapids lettuce.*

wettings. If the edges of the beds dry more quickly, spot watering is recommended to maintain uniform soil moisture.

Watering should be done so that the soil surface is wet for but a brief time to reduce the incidence of diseases (Fig. 96) such as mildew or bottom rot (*Sclerotina* sp.). Air circulation and proper ventilation are encouraged to reduce leaf and stem diseases. Most growers stop watering the crop when the plants cover the rows.

Developments parallel with those for tomatoes have occurred in the use of the nutrient film technique for greenhouse lettuce production—both for Bibb and Grand Rapids types. Essentially, the same nutrient composition is effective for both crops. Growth of lettuce utilizing the nutrient film technique is simplified compared to that for tomatoes, since little physical plant support is required.

⊚   *Temperature.* Lettuce is a cool season crop and does best at fairly low growing temperatures. Optimum day and night temperatures for greenhouse lettuce will vary with variety, age of plant, season, amount of sunlight, and carbon dioxide. High temperatures favor rapid growth, and in the early fall often produce spindly and lightweight plants. During the early stages of plant development, high temperatures have less detrimental effect than if the plants are older. Air circulation is reduced if the plants are large.

The following is recommended for both Bibb and Grand Rapids lettuce production. For both types, a difference of 10 to 15°F temperature between day and night should be maintained. Seedlings on benches should be grown about 5 degrees warmer than older plants in beds. Bibb types should be grown at about 58° at night and 62–68° on cloudy days, and at 70–75° on bright days. Grand Rapids types should be maintained at 50–55° at night and 55–70° during the day, depending on the available light. The greater the amount of sunlight, the higher should be the temperature.

After irrigation when the foilage is wet, it is important to maintain the temperature a few degrees lower than if the foliage was dry and the humidity low. Temperatures should be held as low as possible as the crop nears maturity. This may be difficult, if the greenhouses are not partitioned.

High temperatures in the early spring, even for a short time, will often result in burning of the leaf tip or margin. Proper ventilation for temperature control is essential to prevent this physiological disorder.

⊚   *Cultivation.* Weed control is usually not a problem for greenhouse lettuce, if the soil has been properly sterilized. Shallow cultivation will break up the surface crust, and may be beneficial when the plants are small and the soil is considerably heavy. Cultivation should be limited to small plants. It may do more damage than good when plants begin to cover the row. Cultivation is done with a long handled tool with three or four bent prongs spaced an inch apart.

⊚   *Light, Shade, and Intercropping.* Incoming light into the typical greenhouse environment in mid-winter often does not exceed 1000 to 1200 foot candles. Good growth, however, may occur at as low as 500. Lettuce is well adapted to greenhouse culture during the cloudy days of mid-winter in the northern United States, Europe, and Asia.

The data in Table 39 suggest that under low light conditions the growth of Bibb lettuce is much greater than for Grand Rapids. Since similar dull conditions exist in northern Europe during the winter, the English variety Cheshunt 5–B was hybridized with Bibb to obtain the variety Chesibb which matures 10–14 days earlier than Bibb.

Bibb as an intercrop not only has the same light requirements as tomatoes, but appears more tolerant to shade than Grand Rapids, and does not become spindly. The low growth habit and rapid maturity of Bibb also reduces to a minimum competition with the tomato crop. The variety Domineer used as an intercrop does not elongate as Grand Rapids.

Bolting or seed stalk formation results from long days and high temperatures. Bibb and Grand Rapids are, accordingly, not grown in the greenhouses in late spring and early summer. The variety Domineer has been grown as a late summer crop in plastic houses successfully and in glasshouses in early fall without elongation and bolting.

⊚   *Use of Carbon Dioxide.* Lettuce is perhaps the most responsive to carbon dioxide of all the greenhouse vegetables. Growth of greenhouse lettuce in winter where the ventilators are seldom open during the daylight hours, results in depletion of carbon dioxide within the greenhouse atmosphere. The normal atmosphere contains about 330 ppm of carbon dioxide. However, with an actively grow-

TABLE 39. Comparative responses of Grand Rapids and Bibb lettuce to low light intensities.

Light intensities (foot candles)	Grand Rapids H–54		Bibb	
	(Relative fresh weights of tops)			
	Experiment			
	I	II	I	II
375	39	49	72	115
750	57	125	96	299
1125	105	85	121	154
1500	108	84	108	130

ing crop in closed houses, carbon dioxide levels quickly fall below 200 ppm. It has been demonstrated that artificially increasing the level of carbon dioxide three to six times results in a rapid growth rate and significantly earlier maturity and higher yields.

It is usually not economical to install a carbon dioxide generator if it is to be used for only one crop. However, if several crops are grown, or if a greenhouse is to be used for other crops, it would be profitable to use one. There are several sources of carbon dioxide; natural or propane gas, paraffin (kerosene), or diesel fuel, or pure carbon dioxide. The costs for each source is variable and should be investigated.

Lettuce is not injured as is the tomato from toxic gases emitted as by-products of combustion units in carbon dioxide generation. Although high humidity results from combustion and reduced greenhouse ventilation, lettuce is not subject to fungus diseases as is the tomato. In many ways, greenhouse grown lettuce is the ideal crop for carbon dioxide enrichment. In addition to the information above, it is the standard vegetable for mid-winter production, and good growth occurs at low light intensities and low temperatures.

Information gathered at the Michigan Agricultural Experiment Station on the advantages in the usage of carbon dioxide for greenhouse lettuce is summarized as follows.

I. Crop maturity is hastened (Fig. 97). This will vary from 10 days to several weeks. One practical implication is that an extra crop can be grown during the same growing season.

II. Yields have been increased from 40 to 100 percent (Tables 40–41) when factors such as temperatures, soil fertility levels

Figure 97. *Greenhouse lettuce shows a remarkable response to atmospheric carbon dioxide enrichment. Left to right; Grand Rapids—1000–1500 ppm CO_2, Grand Rapids—normal CO_2, Bibb—normal CO_2, Bibb—1000–1500 ppm CO_2).*

and water are adjusted to take advantage of added carbon dioxide.

III. Carbon dioxide complements the effect of reduced winter light. Yield increases can be obtained in winter production even when light is a limiting factor for plant growth.

IV. Varieties differ greatly in response to carbon dioxide enrichment. Yield increases for rapidly growing Bibb and Cheshunt 5–B were less than for the slower growing Grand Rapids.

V. The dry matter content is generally increased (Table 42).

The following suggestions are made as a guide in the use of carbon dioxide for increasing yield and quality of greenhouse lettuce.

TABLE 40. Yields of lettuce varieties and their selections as modified by the carbon dioxide concentration in the greenhouse atmosphere and the nitrate nitrogen level in the soil (Jan. 5–Feb. 20).

Variety	Weight in lbs/10 heads [a]			Percent increase [a]	
	Normal [b]	$+CO_2$ [b]	$+CO_2$ [b] $+N$ [c]	$+CO_2$	$+CO_2$ $+N$
Bibb	1.5	2.0	2.2	33	47
Summer Bibb	1.3	1.7	2.0	31	54
Buttercrunch	1.4	1.9	1.9	36	36
Cheshunt 5–B	1.6	2.9	3.1	81	94
Cheshunt 5–B x Bibb Selections	1.6	2.2	2.4	38	50
Grand Rapids H–54	1.8	3.3	3.6	83	100
Grand Rapids H–54 x Chestnut 5–B Selections	3.8	5.5	5.6	45	47

[a] Each value an average of two replications.
[b] Normal Co_2 level was approximately 320 ppm; $+CO_2$ level was 1200–1800 ppm.
[c] $+N$ was 100 lbs/acre of ammonium nitrate (NH_1NO_3) applied weekly, resulting in 40 to 50 lbs/acre of available N as NO_3 in the soil. Soils not supplied with the additional nitrogen showed an average test value of 20 lbs/acre of N as nitrate (NO_3) nitrogen.

    I. Higher day and perhaps night temperatures (10–15 degrees day and 5 degrees at night) should be maintained. This will not only increase growth, but tends to avoid excess red pigmentation of Bibb lettuce leaves which often occurs at high carbon dioxide levels.

    II. Fertilizer application, especially nitrogen, should be increased. Recommended levels for N as nitrate nitrogen (NO_3) in the soil should be 40 to 50 pounds per acre.

    III. Watering should be heavier and more frequent.

    IV. Combine carbon dioxide introduction into the houses with an air circulation system.

    ◉ *Air Circulation and Carbon Dioxide.* Studies with carbon dioxide enrichment of greenhouse atmospheres has forcibly drawn attention to an important advantage of air circulation systems. Air

TABLE 41. Yields of lettuce varieties and their selection as an intercrop with greenhouse tomatoes as modified by the carbon dioxide concentration in the greenhouse atmosphere and the nitrate nitrogen level in the soil (Feb. 20–April 2).

Variety	Weight in lbs/10 heads [a]			Percent increase [a]	
	Normal [b]	$+CO_2$ [b]	$+CO_2$ $+N$ [c]	$+CO_2$	$+CO_2$ $+N$
Bibb	1.8	2.0	2.6	11	44
Cheshunt 5–B	2.6	2.8	4.0	8	54
Cheshunt 5–B x					
Bibb Selections	2.9	3.3	3.7	14	28
Grand Rapids H–54	3.3	4.8	7.4	45	124
Grand Rapids—					
Waldmann's Green	3.4	6.4	8.4	88	147
Grand Rapids H–54 x					
Cheshunt 5–B					
Selections	4.7	5.7	7.1	21	51

[a] Each value an average of two replications.
[b] Normal CO_2 level was approximately 320 ppm; $+CO_2$ level was 1200–1800 ppm.
[c] $+N$ was 100 lbs/acre of ammonium nitrate (NH_4NO_3) applied weekly, resulting in 40 to 50 lbs/acre of available N as NO_3 in the soil. Soils not supplied with the additional nitrogen fertilizer showed an average test value of 20 lbs/acre of N as nitrate (NO_3) nitrogen.

TABLE 42. Dry matter content of greenhouse-grown lettuce as influenced by carbon dioxide enrichment and nitrogen fertilization (Feb. 20–April 2).

Variety	Percent dry weight [a]		
	Normal	$+CO_2$ [b]	$+CO_2$ [b] $+N$ [c]
Bibb	3.7	3.6	3.5
Cheshunt 5–B	3.0	3.5	3.6
Grand Rapids H–54	3.6	4.5	3.7

[a] Each value an average of two replications.
[b] Normal CO_2 level was approximately 320 ppm; $+CO_2$ level was 1200–1800 ppm.
[c] $+N$ was 100 lbs/acre of ammonium nitrate (NH_4NO_3 applied weekly, resulting in 40 to 50 lbs/acre of available N as NO_3 in the soil. Soils not supplied with the additional nitrogen fertilizer showed an average test value of 20 lbs/acre of N as nitrate (NO_3) nitrogen.

movement through, or over, plant foliage will reduce the gas diffusion resistance near leaf surfaces. Turbulence maintains a higher carbon dioxide level at the leaf surface. The enclosed atmosphere of a greenhouse is an ideal environment for not only adding carbon dioxide, but for keeping its level high at the photosynthetic site.

Air is drawn directly from a carbon dioxide generating source, placed either within or outside the greenhouse, but preferably on the outside. It is then forced with fans through inflated polyethylene tubes or sleeves that extend the length of the greenhouse. The tubes are perforated at regular intervals, and so oriented that there is good distribution of the added carbon dioxide. The air movement generated will reduce the relative humidity of the atmosphere at the leaf surface, increase the carbon dioxide concentration, and maintain a more uniform temperature. There is value, in the production of lettuce, in circulating the air within a greenhouse as outlined above, even in the absence of carbon dioxide enrichment.

⊛ *New Culture Techniques.* Both Bibb and Grand Rapids types of leaf lettuce may be grown by the several cultures outlined for tomatoes. Most greenhouse lettuce is still grown in standard soil and sand cultures. Peat, peat-lite mixes, and various hydroponic arrangements, including the Nutrient Film Technique (NFT), are now being used. Programming of various cultural operations and planned daily production of a standardized product has been achieved. Production around the calendar according to a blueprint is now possible under controlled environment facilities. This is true for installations that now exist in both the United States and Europe. Many different lettuce varieties and types of Dutch origin respond. The Nutrient Film Technique (NFT) and the related Hygro-Flo(TM) systems have been adapted for greenhouse lettuce culture (Fig. 98). The same nutrient formulation as for tomatoes may be used. With all hydroponic cultures, including NFT, carbon dioxide enrichment of greenhouse atmospheres to a level of 1000 ppm gives highly significant yield increases.

As to the future, continued research and development will be necessary. New varieties and cultural techniques will be forthcoming. One of the very latest is production on rock wool blocks (Fig. 99). There are still the highly complex engineering problems of climate control. The need still remains for greater mechanization of transplanting and harvesting.

Figure 98. *Lettuce Production utilizing the nutrient film technique. Top, Nutrient Film Technique; bottom, Hygro-Flo* (TM) *System.*

◎ *Harvesting.* Time to maturity of lettuce from transplanting depends upon the season of year and market demand. Smaller lettuce plants are harvested when the price is good. Since greenhouse lettuce is sold by weight, growers try to attain maximum size without

Figure 99. *Rock wool block culture of greenhouse lettuce* (DENMARK, *1978*). *Top, growing seedlings on rock wool blocks in the propagating house; bottom, close-up showing the mat of roots in the block.*

reduction in quality before harvesting. With leaf lettuce 90 or more days is required to obtain proper size during the winter months after transplanting.

Bibb matures 1 to 3 weeks ahead of Grand Rapids, depending

Figure 100. *Grand Rapids (top) and Bibb (bottom) lettuce is hand cut and packed in veneer baskets or water proof cardboard boxes.*

upon the season. Chesibb, a winter variety, matures 10 to 14 days ahead of Bibb. In early fall and late spring, Bibb lettuce may be harvested in 4–5 weeks, and in mid-winter 7–10 weeks, after setting in the beds. Grand Rapids requires 5–6 weeks in the fall, and over 12 weeks in the winter after transplanting.

The lettuce plants are cut just above the soil surface with a

short blade knife, trimmed of yellow leaves, and packed directly
into containers. Harvesting of lettuce is labor intensive (Fig. 100).
Leaf (Grand Rapids type) is packed in 10 pound rectangular splint
boxes or waterproof cardboard cartons. Bibb is either packed in

Figure 101. *Mechanical packaging of lettuce (top) and transport of the packages
in plastic crates (bottom). Note overhead rail system for moving the product*
(DENMARK, *1977*).

18 x 18 x 4 inch or rectangular waterproof cardboard cartons. Ideally, 18 to 20 heads of leaf lettuce are packed in a 10 pound carton and 24 to 30 heads of Bibb are packed in a 5 pound carton. A few growers in western Europe mechanically pack lettuce in special film packages with individual or a group of heads (Fig. 101). The packaging protects the product in transit, and makes it convenient for retail sale. The individual packages are placed in special plastic crates for transport.

⊚   *Yield and Profit.* Profit from a unit area of greenhouse space is dependent upon market demand, price, quality, yield, labor, fuel, fertilizer, and other production costs. The price for a 5 pound carton of Bibb is generally the same as that for a 10 pound carton of Grand Rapids leaf lettuce. Yield depends upon the stage of plant development prior to harvest. A conservative yield is 10 pounds of leaf and 5 pounds of Bibb per 10 square feet of greenhouse space.

The returns from greenhouse grown lettuce are reflected by the price of outdoor grown head lettuce. Shortages of head lettuce may greatly accelerate the price of greenhouse lettuce—both Bibb and Grand Rapids. This occurred in the U.S.A. during the spring of 1978, when prices for greenhouse grown lettuce received by the producer exceeded $1.00 per pound.

LETTUCE LITERATURE

Anonymous. *Salad and Other Food Crops in Glasshouses*. Ministry of Agriculture, Fisheries and Food. Bulletin No. 143. United Kingdom Her Majesty's Stationary Office, London. 1963.

Anonymous. *Bean Bros. Build Up Vast Yorks Lettuce Factory*. The Grower, pp. 283, 284, 289. January 30, 1971.

Bert, J. S., Jr. and S. Honma. *Effect of Soil Moisture and Irrigation Method on Tipburn and Edgeburn Severity in Greenhouse Lettuce*. Jour. Amer. Soc. Hort. Science 100(3):278–282. 1975.

Hafen, Leslie. *Bibb and Leaf Lettuce in Plastic Greenhouses*. Purdue University Agricultural Extension Service. Mimeo HO–61–1.

Honma, S. and S. H. Wittwer. *Chesibb—A New Butterhead Lettuce for the Greenhouse and Outdoor Plantings*. Michigan Agricultural Experiment Station Research Report 85. 1969.

Honma, S. and S. H. Wittwer. *Domineer—A New Greenhouse Lettuce*. Michigan Agricultural Experiment Station Research Report 163. 1972.

Kuiken, J. C. and G. H. Germing. *All the Year Round Lettuce Production*. Span. 15(2):89–91, 1972.

Large, J. G. *Glasshouse Lettuce*. Grower Books, 49 Doughty Street, London WC 1N 2 LP. 1972.

Shippers, P. A. *The Mechanization of Dutch lettuce*. American Vegetable Grower, pp. 40, 42. December, 1977.

Thompson, R. C. *Growing Lettuce in Greenhouses*. United States Department of Agriculture. Agriculture Handbook No. 149. 1958.

Tiessen, H., J. Wiebe, and C. Fisher. *Greenhouse Vegetable Production in Ontario*. Ontario Ministry of Agriculture and Food Publication 526. Toronto, Canada. 1976.

Wittwer, S. H., S. Honma and W. Robb. *Practices for Increasing Yields of Greenhouse Lettuce*. Michigan Agricultural Experiment Station Research Report 22. 1964.

❧ GREENHOUSE CUCUMBERS

❧ INTRODUCTION

The production of greenhouse cucumbers in many parts of the world parallels that of greenhouse tomatoes. The cucumber is a semi-tropical vegetable, and grows best under conditions of high light, humidity, moisture, temperature, and fertilizer. Its growth habit, similar to the tomato, is indeterminate. It will produce fruit continuously where disease and insects are controlled. The cucumber, however, is more sensitive than the tomato to low temperatures, which can cause reductions in both growth and yield.

The cucumber is almost always grown in rotation with lettuce and tomatoes, or in rotation with bedding or vegetable plants. It is possible to grow cucumbers after greenhouses become empty in the spring following bedding plant production.

Growing of greenhouse cucumbers can be a profitable business for progressive growers. However, as with tomatoes and lettuce, it requires practical know-how and technical knowledge. The production of a quality product is an exact and expensive venture, involving high technology. Recent large scale ventures in the comparative production of greenhouse tomatoes and cucumbers suggest it is easier to successfully grow cucumbers than tomatoes. The fuel costs are, however, greater with cucumbers than tomatoes.

❧ PROTECTED STRUCTURES

Greenhouse structures described for the growing of tomatoes and lettuce can be used for the growing of cucumbers, with a slight modification in heating systems. Cucumbers require a higher temperature for satisfactory growth.

Sandy loam soils, high in organic matter, are preferable. The roots of the cucumber plant require good aeration. A system of drainage is essential, and the same drainage tiles can be used for steam sterilization. To maintain a loose friable soil, organic matter—such as rotted manure, chopped hay, peanut hulls—must be added once a year. Fresh organic materials should not be added to the soil, since they may cause nitrogen deficiency of the crop. The soil should be well fertilized and tilled, and ridges built prior to planting.

ࣷ VARIETIES

Prior to the introduction of European seedless cucumbers, the standard greenhouse varieties grown in North America were those developed for field production such as Burpee Hybrid, Highmoor, etc. These standard or North American varieties are 7–10 inches long, of fairly uniform width throughout the length, thick-skinned, and dark green with light green mottled stripes. The flowers of these varieties must be pollinated by bees to set fruits. The fruits, therefore, contain well developed seeds when picked for market, and are indistinguishable from field grown types. Very few, if any, of these cucumbers are now grown in the United States or Europe.

The long seedless European cucumber has, in recent years, replaced the North American varieties. Plantings are found in Canada, California, Arizona, and Ohio. It is a product that originated from European greenhouses. The fruits of the European types are seedless, 12–20 inches long, have a slightly wrinkled surface, slightly ridged lengthwise, uniformly green, non-bitter, thin skinned, and usually have a short neck on the stem end (Fig. 102, 103). No peeling is required before eating. The thin skinned fruit is either waxed or shrink-wrapped to prevent excessive moisture loss. The cucumber is parthenocarpic and sets fruit without pollination. Pollination in these types should be avoided, since it causes seed development, and the fruit becomes clubbed at the blossom end and develops a bitter taste.

There are three types of the European seedless cucumber. They are sub-divided by the flowering habit: (1) the *all female,* which produces only female or pistillate flowers; (2) the *gynoecious,* which is predominantly female with some male or staminate flowers appearing; (3) the *monecious,* which has both male and female flowers.

Figure 102. *Top, European seedless cucumber in experimental greenhouse at Michigan State University, East Lansing (Spring 1975). Bottom, cucumbers packed for marketing* (DENMARK, JULY, 1977).

All of these three types produce fruit parthenocarpically, but the monecious and predominantly female can produce seeds and, therefore, bees must be kept out of the greenhouses or the male flowers

Figure 103. *Top, European seedless cucumber. (State Farm Moscow, USSR. July, 1977). Bottom, European seedless cucumber. Al Gerhart—Cleveland, Ohio (March, 1978).*

should be removed as soon as they become visible and prior to opening. The monecious types, which continuously produce male or staminate flowers, are not recommended. Predominantly female types can be used with confidence. The few male flowers that develop, however, should be removed. The all female type is recommended, since they produce no male flowers. Listed below is a partial list of F_1 hybrid cucumber varieties grouped by flowering habit. Growers are encouraged to test these new hybrids with their own, or other local varieties.

All female	Predominantly female	Monecious
Bambina	Brilliant	Bitspot
Corpora	Fortuna	Cresta
Famosa	Dipinix	Green Spot
Farbio	Princess	Green Stick
Farbiola	Stero	Picador
Fela	Toska	Sporu
Femdan		
Femspot		
Fertila		
Herta		
La Reine		
Minisol		
Monique		
Pandex		
Sandra		
Uniflora		
Virgo		

ॐ PEST CONTROL

European types of cucumbers have shown little resistance to diseases. Some of the varieties have resistance to scab (*Cladosporium cucumerinium*) and to leaf spot (*Cercospora melonis*). Varieties resistant to powdery mildew are being developed. They are also subject to the same insect problems as the standard American seeded types. Both red spider mites and white fly can be controlled biologically by appropriate use of parasites and natural predators as described for tomatoes.

৪ PLANT GROWING

Cucumber plants are grown in peat pots, soil or peat blocks, Kys-Kubes [33] or BR-8 blocks [34], or in clay or plastic pots. The soil or soil mix used for the pots should be properly sterilized before seeding, and the seed treated with a fungicide to prevent damping-off. One or more seeds are placed in the pot and, when the plants are properly established, are pinched to one plant per pot. Temperature during germination should be near 80°F (28°C) and after germination at 70° (21°C). Plants should be grown rapidly, with no check in growth. Additional fertilizer may be needed toward the end of the growing period. Nitrogen, at a rate of 1¼ lbs. of ammonium nitrate in 1 gallon of water and diluted to 1:200, should be fed to the seedlings.

⊛ *Light.* For early spring crops, supplemental light for the young seedlings is desirable. Cucumbers, in the early seedling stage, respond to supplemental light. Day length should be extended to 12–14 hours with 1,800–2,000 foot candles at the plant level. Plants should be progressively spaced as they grow to avoid crowding and becoming spindly. Leaves of adjacent plants should not touch. For the spring crop, approximately a 5 week growing period from seeding (mid-winter) is required; and for the fall crop, a 4 week period (mid-summer) is needed prior to transplanting.

⊛ *Temperature Requirements.* Plant growing temperatures between 80 to 85°F with plenty of sunlight are ideal for good growth. Minimum temperatures should not be lower than 70° during the day or night. In the fall, some heat must be provided if the outside temperature falls below 60°.

⊛ *Planting and Spacing.* Plants are placed in permanent beds at the 4–5 leaf stage, or before they become pot bound. Approximately four square feet per plant are required for the North American varieties. Generally, two rows are spaced 30 inches apart, and then an

---

33 Keyes Fiber Co., 160 Summit Avenue, Montvale, New Jersey 07645.
34 Famco, Inc., 300 Lake Road, Medina, Ohio 44256.

alley of 40 inches provided between the pair of rows to allow for working space. Plants in the row are spaced 16–18 inches apart. For the European types, 7–9 square feet per plant for the spring crop, and 9–10 square feet per plant for the fall crop are desired. The increased space for fall grown crops will compensate for the shorter daylength and less intense sunlight. A minimum of 5 feet between rows, and a 20 inch spacing within the row is advised.

◉   *Carbon Dioxide Enrichment.* Enrichment of the greenhouse atmosphere with carbon dioxide up to 1500 ppm both in the seedling and permanent growing area will increase growth and yield by 25 to 50 percent. In the winter, carbon dioxide is introduced beginning with sunrise and continued until one to two hours before sunset. In the spring and early fall with the need for ventilation, the enrichment period is shortened, since the carbon dioxide escapes through the opened vents. All details of carbon dioxide enrichment outlined for tomatoes and lettuce apply to cucumbers.

◉   *Mulching.* Mulching is suggested for cucumbers. Straw, hay, peanut hulls, or corncobs are placed in the alternate or wide rows. The mulch reduces soil water evaporation, soil compaction, and soil temperature fluctuations. The decaying organic matter also liberates carbon dioxide, which promotes increased growth.

◉   *Training and Trimming.* The plants are trained upwards so that the main stem is allowed to climb to the overhead wire along a polyethylene twine. Wires are attached 6 to 7 feet above the ground. The use of the V-cordon system is advised to make use of available light in the greenhouse. Two top wires are spaced $2\frac{1}{2}$ to 3 feet apart above the single row of plants. The twine for each plant is alternately tied to the overhead wires. This will incline the plants away from the row on each side, thus creating a better light receiving system.

The main stem is pruned to one leaf above the overhead wire, and the plant is tied below the leaf to the wire to prevent it from sliding down the twine. No fruit is allowed to develop on the main stem up to $4\frac{1}{2}$ feet. All laterals are removed that appear for the first 2 feet. For the next 2 feet, the laterals are allowed to produce one leaf and then the growing tip pruned. In the third 2 feet, laterals are allowed to produce 2 leaves and are stopped. The two top laterals are trained over the wire in a canopy fashion or umbrella

method and hung alongside the main stem to about ½ or ⅔ of
the way down. On these, the developing laterals are stopped after
2 leaves (Fig. 104). This method of training is somewhat more complex than the much simpler system now recommended (Fig. 105).

Pruning of each plant is based on plant vigor and fruit load. Extensive leaf growth is prevented to allow proper coloring of the
fruits. The development of the fruit is dependent on the continuing
production of leaf axils. If too many fruits are set at once, fruit
thinning is necessary to avoid malformed and non-marketable small
fruit. Such fruit, as they appear, should be removed. Multiple fruits
on an axil should be thinned to one. Weak unproductive laterals
should be removed.

⊚ *Fertilizer Schedule.* Similar to the greenhouse tomato, the
cucumber requires a proper balance of nutrients to produce a good
crop. It has a high fertilizer requirement; therefore, constant high
levels of nutrients are required. Where organic matter is lacking,
50–70 tons per acre of well rotted manure should be worked into the
soil prior to sterilization. If the soil is low in phosphorus and potash,
1,000 to 2,000 pounds per acre of 0–20–20 should be added after
sterilization, and rototilled into the soil prior to planting. After the
plants are set in the ground, the plants are watered with a starter
solution (10–52–17), equivalent to ½ to one ounce per gallon of
water.

The fertilizer schedule listed in Table 43 is a guide. Growers
should adapt it to their local growing conditions. Soil and tissue tests
should be made periodically, when possible. Common sense and
good judgment should govern the amount of fertilizer used. The
amount of fertilizer suggested is based on a study made at the Research Station, Harrow, Ontario, Canada. A cucumber crop population of 8840 plants per acre grown from January 15 to July 15
produced 27 pounds of fruit per plant. This crop removed from the
soil the following amounts of nutrients per acre: 364 pounds of
nitrogen, 82 pounds of phosphorus, 490 pounds of potassium, 212
pounds of calcium, and 51 pounds of magnesium.

Where soil and tissue tests show a shortage of magnesium, or
plant symptoms from a previous crop indicate a deficiency, incorpo-
rate 200–250 pounds of magnesium sulfate into the soil prior to
planting. If magnesium deficiency should appear on the crop, the
plants should be either sprayed with 5 pounds magnesium sulfate

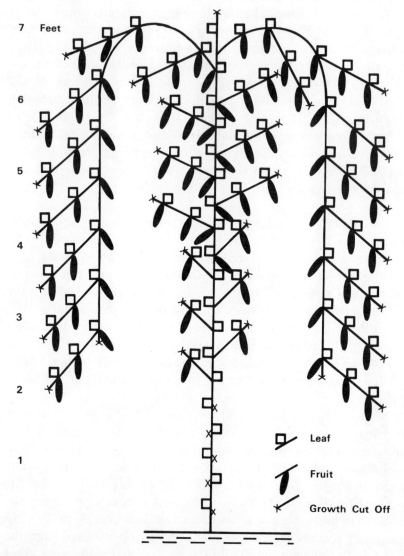

Figure 104. *Complex system for training of European cucumbers* (COURTESY OF ARTHUR LOUGHTON, DIRECTOR OF THE HORTICULTURAL EXPERIMENT STATION, SIMCOE, ONTARIO, CANADA N3Y 4N5).

in 100 gallons of water, or 80 pounds of magnesium sulfate applied per acre in a water solution to the soil. Repeat the application, as needed.

⊛ *Watering.* Cucumbers have a high water requirement. Periodically, heavy watering is desirable to ensure proper penetration to

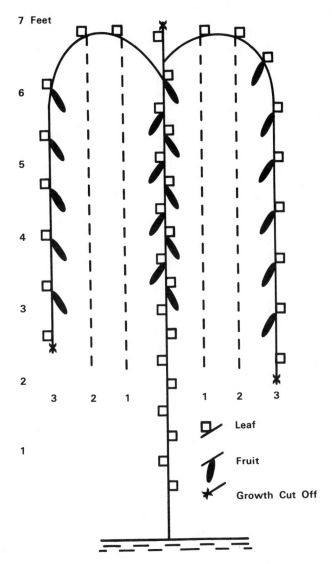

Figure 105. *Simplified and recommended system for training greenhouse-grown European cucumbers* (COURTESY OF ARTHUR LOUGHTON, DIRECTOR OF THE HORTI-CULTURAL EXPERIMENT STATION, SIMCOE, ONTARIO, CANADA N3Y 4N5; AND FRANK INGRATTA, VINELAND HORTICULTURAL STATION, VINELAND, ONTARIO, CANADA L0R 2E0).

the root zone. Warm water (not below 65°F) should be used in irrigating. Cold water chills the roots, and will slow plant growth with a direct reduction in yield. During the warm spring and early summer, the leaves of cucumber plants should be sprinkled lightly to increase the humidity of the greenhouse and reduce water loss from the plant. This practice should be limited to the early part of

TABLE 43. Suggested weekly fertilizer schedule for greenhouse cucumber production in soil culture.

| | Fertilizer (pounds per acre) | | | | Nutrients supplied (pounds per acre) | | |
Week	Ammonium nitrate	Calcium nitrate	Potassium nitrate	Diammo-nium phosphate	N	P	K
1–3		40	50	20	14	10	22
4–10	80	40	70	20	43	10	31
11–18	130	40	70	20	60	10	31

the day, and should be terminated in time so that the leaves dry by nightfall. This will promote good growth and, at the same time, reduce incidence of mildew, *Botrytis*, and other leaf and stem diseases.

ଛ NEW TYPES OF CULTURE

Greenhouse cucumbers, in addition to being grown in regular greenhouse soils, may be produced on straw bales (Figs. 106, 107), in peat modules, troughs and bolsters, on rock wool (Fig. 108), with artificial mixes, the nutrient film technique (NFT) (Fig. 109), Hygro-Flo(TM) systems, and sand culture (Fig. 110). In each of these methods of culture, a slight modification from the nutrient requirements of the tomato is necessary.

⊛   *Straw Bale Culture.* This method of culture has been found more desirable for cucumbers than for tomatoes. Straw bale culture was first developed and practiced for successful greenhouse cucumber production in western Europe. One of the advantages is the release of carbon dioxide from the decaying straw. Straw bale culture can also be used where greenhouse soils are chemically contaminated. The decaying straw also provides a higher root temperature. Straw free from slow decomposing herbicides should be used. Even the slightest residue is sufficient to kill the cucumber plant after transplanting.

Figure. 106. *Cucumber production in the United Kingdom. Straw bale culture in the background.*

Figure 107. *Straw bale culture in Denmark. Note top and center, white plastic cover over bale for heat conservation and light reflection. Bottom, note pulling of plant as bale decreases in size from straw decomposition.*

Figure 108. *Straw bale culture in Denmark. Top, note drip hose placed next to each plant. Bottom, rock wool mat with root distribution.*

Details of culture are as follows. Wheat straw bales are placed end to end in 3–6 inch trenches, or flat on the ground on poly-ethylene film that is a foot wider than the bales. The bales are soaked with water before fertilizers are applied. The amount of water applied per bale depends upon the condition of the straw, whether

Figure 109. *Nutrient Film Technique (NFT) experimental plantings of cucumbers. Glasshouse Crops Research Institute, Littlehampton, England (July, 1977). Top, Drs. G. W. Winsor (left) and A. J. Cooper (right).*

new or weathered. The average is 15 gallons per bale. Following three to four days of daily watering, 5–6 ounces of ammonium nitrate is applied per 40 lb. bale. This is followed by several days of daily watering. On the 7th and the 10th days, an additional 3 ounces of ammonium nitrate is applied. The bales are watered daily. Superphosphate and potassium nitrate at 10 ounces each are applied along with magnesium sulfate at 3 ounces, and 2 ounces of ferrous sulfate per bale on the 10th day. Water is applied daily to the bale until the plants are ready to set. The temperature of the bales may internally rise to 120 to 140°F. Planting should not begin until temperature drops below 100°F. If phosphate and potash are omitted during the fermentation process, these nutrients must be supplied to the plants soon after transplanting as a liquid feed.

Prior to planting the cucumber plant, a small bed of soil (top cap) is placed on the bale deep enough to take the ball of roots of the transplant. The top cap is made up of equal parts of sterilized loam and peat, and 1–2 pounds of ground limestone per bale. In Western Europe, white polyethylene is placed over the straw bales, and a hole is made over the soil cap for the transplant (Fig. 107). The transplants are supplied liquid fertilizer through drip hoses. For the first three weeks, 5 ounces of ammonium nitrate in one gallon of water diluted to 1:200 is applied three times a week. From the third to the sixth week, 12 ounces of ammonium nitrate in one gallon of water and diluted to 1:200 is applied at every watering.

Figure 110. *Commercial sand culture of greenhouse cucumbers—Superior Farming Company, Inc., Tucson, Arizona. 1976.*

From the 7th week to the end of crop, 8 ounces of ammonium nitrate, 2 ounces of potassium nitrate, and 2 ounces of magnesium sulfate per gallon of water diluted to 1:200 is applied three times a week.

For plants trained to the cordon system of culture, it is especially important for plants grown on straw bales to keep the twine slack enough to prevent the roots from being pulled from the soil, as the bales deteriorate and sink as the season progresses (Fig. 107).

A modified straw bale culture for the growing of cucumbers is being used by the West of Scotland Agricultural College. This system requires a continuous liquid feeding, and removes the use of solid fertilizer and the need for an initial straw breakdown period. Straw bales on polyethylene are watered with a 2:1:2 liquid feed diluted to a conductivity factor (CF) of 16 (1.6 mmhos). Frequent small feeding of the liquid is made to the bales for a period of 10 to 14 days until the bales are well soaked. The bales are then top capped 5–6 inches deep, and transplants placed in them.

The liquid feeding begins 2 weeks later with the same fertilizer solution diluted to a CF of 8 (0.8 mmhos). Four to five weeks after transplanting, the concentration of the solution should be increased to CF of 16 and continued to the end of the crop.

⊛ *Peat Culture.* The technique for growing cucumbers in straw bale culture parallels that for peat substrates, such as beds or bolsters. There is a difference in nutrient requirement. Cucumber plants in peat cultures require more nitrogen and supplementary applications of lime, potash, and phosphate 4–5 weeks after transplanting. It is not easy to overcome the problem of lowering the potash and phosphorus levels by adding more to the base fertilizer for peat. Cucumbers are very sensitive to high salts. An excess will result in root damage.

Cucumbers grown in a peat substrate require large amounts of nitrogen in the early stages of growth to obtain the rapid growth desired. When heavy fruiting begins, high amounts of nitrogen and potassium are required with only a moderate amount of phosphorus. Growers are reluctant to add phosphorus because of possible blockage of the drip nozzles. If the phosphorus is fed separately, and the lines washed, the plugging will be lessened.

It is recommended that 300 ppm of nitrogen and potassium be applied in the irrigation water for the first four weeks, then increased to 375 ppm from the 5th to 12th week, and dropped to 300 ppm until the end of the crop. Beginning the 5th week, 100 ppm of phosphorus should be added in a ratio of 1 part of phosphorus to 4 parts of nitrogen and potassium. This will prevent a deficiency of phosphorus.

Cucumber seedlings planted in peat, whether in bags or troughs, should be started dry and gradually wetted. It is important to avoid over wetting the peat before or soon after planting. This can result in chilling the plants, or cause them to stand in free water.

◉ *Rock Wool Culture*. There is an increasing use of rock wool marketed as "Grodan" [35] in growing greenhouse cucumbers in western Europe. Plants are started in $1\frac{1}{2}$ inch rock wool blocks with a small hole on the top. The cucumber seed is placed in the hole, and granulated rock wool is used to cover the seed to prevent washing out. The blocks are placed on a slightly sloping surface covered with plastic sheeting. A basic nutrient solution of 2 percent nitrogen, 11 percent phosphate, 40 percent potassium, 5 percent magnesium oxide and trace elements is required. The blocks are soaked with a solution containing 1.9 grams of the basic solution and 1.9 grams of nitrate limestone (calcium nitrate) in one gallon of water. As the seeds germinate, 2.85 grams of the basic solution and 3.42 grams of the nitrate limestone are dissolved in a gallon of water and are applied to the blocks.

As the plants begin to grow, the blocks are spaced so that the leaves do not touch each other. To prevent over watering and the possibility of slowing down the growth, the wetness of the blocks must be checked frequently. Pythium infection can be avoided by maintaining temperatures above 68°F by using bottom heat and warm water for irrigation.

The plants are placed in the middle of rock wool slabs at the 3 to 5 leaf stage, and a drip nozzle accommodates each plant block (Fig. 108). The slabs or mats are laid end to end on polyethylene sheets that are a foot wider than the blocks. The polyethylene is wrapped around the side and the top.

In fertilizing the cucumber plants on the rockwool slabs or mats, the fertilizer solution and irrigation water together should approximate the nutrient concentration as shown:

[35] Grodania A/S, Hovedgarden 495, DK 2640, Hedehusene, Denmark.

Conductivity value   2–3 mmhos—pH 6.5

Nitrogen	180 ppm	Sulfur	30 ppm
Phosphorus	30 ppm	Iron	2 ppm
Potassium	190 ppm	Magnesium	1.5 ppm
Magnesium	30 ppm	Boron	0.2 ppm
Calcium	120 ppm		

It is necessary to sample the nutrient levels in the rock wool mats several times a week, and to monitor the conductivity value of the solution. A concentration of 1.7–2.0 mmhos should be maintained. Irrigate 1–4 times a day. Irrigation should be terminated when dripping from the mats starts. Occasionally, some leaching should occur to avoid accumulation of excess soluble salts in the rock wool.

⊛ *Nutrient Film Technique (NFT).* This new method, along with the Hygro-Flo⁽ᵀᴹ⁾ system of hydroponic culture, has the same advantages and limitations for growing greenhouse cucumbers as for tomatoes or lettuce. Developments at the Glasshouse Crops Research Institute at Littlehampton in the United Kingdom with cucumbers have paralleled those of tomatoes (Fig. 109). Nutrient formulations similar to those outlined earlier for lettuce and tomatoes are satisfactory. Heating the water to raise the root temperatures may prove beneficial. The design specifications outlined for greenhouse tomatoes can be followed.

⊛ *Grafting.* Where root diseases such as *Fusarium* and Corky-root are present in the soil, cucumber seedlings of the desired variety and type may be grafted onto resistant rootstocks such as *Cucurbita ficifolia*. The practice is common in Japan and western Europe. Seeds of *C. ficifolia* are normally planted 5 to 6 days later than the desired cucumber variety. Seeds of the rootstock should be pregerminated and transplanted into seedling boxes or flats. If there is difficulty in germinating seeds of the rootstock because of a hard seed coat, a small part of the side of the seed should be cut with a razor blade. This allows for the absorption of water. A loose friable soil containing peat and sand is desirable for growing plants of both the scion and the rootstock, since the plants are lifted and transplanted after grafting. Ten to twelve days after germination, the plants of the rootstock are ready to be grafted.

The approach graft has proven successful. Rootstock plants are carefully removed from the seedling flat, and a one-half inch downward incision is made with a razor blade below the first secondary leaf. The scion cucumber plant is carefully lifted, and an upward incision is made approximately at the same height of the incision of the rootstock. The lips of the incision are placed into each other and secured with a strip of adhesive tape. Both plants are then potted together and placed in a high humidity chamber or room for 10–12 days. All but one of the leaves of the rootstock are removed as soon as possible after grafting. The top of the rootstock above the graft and stem of the scion plant below the graft are cut after 10 days.

Grafted plants are earlier, root disease resistant, and produce a larger crop than non-grafted plants. They can also withstand lower soil temperatures. The disadvantages of grafting are the extra labor requirements. Virus diseases are also easily transmitted if a few plants are infected.

◉   *Harvesting.* Fruits are harvested when they are more or less cylindrical and well filled. For the North American types, fruit should be 8–9 inches long, and 2–2¼ inches in diameter. For the European types, cylindrical fruits greater than 11 inches in length should be harvested. European seedless cucumbers, with their thin skins, lose moisture more rapidly than the North American types, and should be shrink-wrapped and stored in a cooler (50–55°F) to retain high quality (Fig. 111).

Figure 111. *Shrink wrapping of Seedless European cucumbers—Superior Farming Company, Inc., Tucson, Arizona. 1976.*

CUCUMBER LITERATURE

Adams, Peter, *How Cucumbers Respond to Variation in Nutrition.* The Grower 89:197, 199, 201. 1978.

Anonymous. *The Big Switch. European Cukes Replace Tomato Crop.* Amer. Veg. Grower 22:13–15. 1974.

Anonymous. *Greenhouse Vegetable Production Recommendations.* Ontario Ministry of Agriculture and Food. Pub. 365. 1977–78.

Duvald, F. *Cucumber Growing Under Glass.* J. E. Ohlsens Enke, DK 2630 Taastrup, Denmark. 1974.

Johnson, Hunter, Jr. *Greenhouse Vegetable Varieties—Tomato and Cucumber.* Agricultural Extension Memo Greenhouse Vegetable Production. November 1973.

Johnson, Hunter, Jr. *Greenhouse Cucumber Production.* University of California Agricultural Extension AXT–M–79. 1972.

Krause, W. *Female Cucumbers Given High Boost by New Developments in Holland.* The Grower 612, 614, 616. March 11, 1972.

Loughton, Arthur. *Growing Long Seedless Cucumbers in Plant-Raising Greenhouses.* Ontario Ministry of Agriculture and Food. Fact sheet AGDEX 292/20. 1971.

Loughton, Arthur. *Growing European Seedless Cucumbers.* Ontario Ministry of Agriculture and Food. Fact sheet AGDEX 292/21. 1972.

Loughton, Arthur. *Straw-Bale Culture of Greenhouse Crops.* Proceedings on International Symposium on Controlled Environment Agriculture. pp. 208–215. Environmental Research Laboratories, University of Arizona, Tucson. 1977.

Loughton, A. and W. A. Straver. *The Culture of Greenhouse Cucumbers on Organic Substrates.* Report of the Horticultural Research Institute of Ontario. pp. 113–123, 1969.

Maher, M. J., W. J. Woods, J. J. Bannon and An Foras Taluntais. *Program for Early Cucumber Production.* Glasshouse and Mushroom Department, Kinsealy, Dublin 5, Ireland. April, 1970.

Roorda van Eysinga, J. P. N. L. and K. W. Smilde. *Nutritional Disorders in Cucumbers and Gherkins Under Glass.* Center for Agricultural Publishing and Documentation. Wageningen, The Netherlands. 1969.

Staver, W. A. *Growing European Seedless Cucumbers.* Horticultural Research Institute of Ontario, Ministry of Agriculture and Food Fact Sheet AGDEX 292/20. 1978.

Tiessen, H., J. Wiebe, and C. Fisher. *Greenhouse Vegetable Production in Ontario.* Ontario Ministry of Agriculture and Food Publication 526. Toronto, Canada. 1976.

Ward, G. M. *Greenhouse Cucumber Nutrition: A Growth Analysis Study*. Plant and Soil 24:324–332. 1967.

Ward, G. M. and J. R. Rainforth. *Fertilizer Schedule for Greenhouse Cucumbers in Southwest Ontario*. Canada Department of Agriculture Pub. 1394. 1969.